SMOKE & MIRRORS:
FINANCIAL MYTHS
THAT WILL RUIN YOUR
RETIREMENT DREAMS

David Trahair, CA

Self-Counsel Press
(a division of)
International Self-Counsel Press Ltd.
Canada   USA

Self-Counsel Press acknowledges the financial support of the Government of Canada through the Book Publishing Industry Development Program (BPIDP) for our publishing activities.

Printed in Canada.

First edition: 2004; Reprinted 2004

Second edition: 2005

Library and Archives Canada Cataloguing in Publication

Trahair, David
    Smoke and mirrors : financial myths that will ruin your retirement dreams / David Trahair. — 2nd ed.

(Self-counsel reference series)
ISBN 1-55180-594-4

1. Finance, Personal. 2. Retirement income. 3. Investments.
I. Title. II. Title: Smoke and mirrors. III. Series.
HG179.T722   2004a   332.024'01   C2004-906174-7

Excerpts from *Personal Financial Planning*, 3rd. ed., by Kwok Ho and Chris Robinson, (Concord, Ontario: Captus Press Inc., 2001). Reprinted with permission of Captus Press Inc., Units 14 & 15, 1600 Steeles Ave. West, Concord, ON L4K 4M2. E-mail: info@captus.com, Internet: http://www.captus.com.

Figure 3, MORTGAGE2 PRO, copyright © 2003 is used by permission of Ron Cirotto.

Figure 5, MORTGAGE2 PRO, copyright © 2003 is used by permission of Ron Cirotto.

Figure 6, MORTGAGE2 PRO, copyright © 2003 is used by permission of Ron Cirotto.

Self-Counsel Press
(a division of)
International Self-Counsel Press Ltd.

1481 Charlotte Road	1704 N. State Street
North Vancouver, BC V7J 1H1	Bellingham, WA 98225
Canada	USA

CONTENTS

CHARTS

FIGURES

WORKSHEETS

ACKNOWLEDGEMENTS

I loved writing this book, but it wasn't produced by me alone. This book is the result of a team effort.

First and foremost, I would like to thank the people at Self-Counsel Press for making this venture such a pleasure. I'd like to start by expressing my sincere gratitude to Judy Brunsek. If not for Judy, this book would not exist. She was the one that showed this rookie writer how to actually get past the idea stage.

I'd also like to thank Richard Day for immediately seeing the potential in my proposal; Catherine Bennett for her precise proofing skills; Aaron Morris for his creative flair; Roger Kettyls for spreading the word so well; and most of all, Ruth Wilson for her brilliant editing. She has a knack for taking a somewhat complex issue and stating it cleanly and elegantly. Because of her, there now exists a simple book on how Canadians can get their finances under control. I will always owe a lot to Ruth.

I'm also indebted to Ron Cirotto for sharing his mortgage know-how and his excellent amortization software; Alan Salmon for his help in making the tools on the CD-ROM more self-explanatory and interactive; and Kwok Ho and Chris Robinson for their excellent book, *Personal Financial Planning*.

Special thanks must go to Dale Ennis, the founder and editor-in-chief of *Canadian MoneySaver* magazine. Dale has beliefs similar to mine about the state of "financial planning" in Canada today and has been instrumental in helping me get the word out.

Last, but not least, I must thank my parents, Peter and Florence, for their never-ending support, and, of course, the lights of my life — my wife, Elaine, and our children, Cassidy and Kyle.

PART ONE

UNDERSTANDING AND EXPLODING FIVE BIG MYTHS OF FINANCIAL PLANNING

1
MEET THE
MYTHS

SEEING THROUGH THE SMOKE AND MIRRORS

You may be wondering, "Another book on financial planning? What more is there to say? Haven't we heard it all?"

In that lies the problem. Each and every day, we are bombarded by messages from so-called financial advisers, the foot soldiers of the big finance companies, imploring us to secure our financial future by giving them control of our personal finances.

You've heard the pitches:

- "Invest with us and retire rich!"

- "Buy life insurance from us and secure your financial future!"

- "Get that loan you need to realize your dreams!"

These pitches are often accompanied by scare tactics: "Don't you know that you'll need millions of dollars stashed away by the time you retire, or you'll be forced to live in a cardboard box, surviving on macaroni and cheese for the rest of your life?"

The truth is that the people who send these messages are pulling the wool over your eyes. Many of them are merely sales people offering advice that will benefit themselves — not you. They are in it simply for the commissions.

Take the big banks, for example. They are not in business to secure your happy retirement. Their objective is to maximize the value of their company to keep their shareholders happy. They do this by maximizing their profit. When you bank, invest, or borrow from them, they are increasing their profit with each and every transaction. Their profit comes from your pocket, and it's eating away at your nest egg each and every hour of every day of your life.

It's time to do something about it all. Something needs to be said to clear the air — to help you — and all Canadians — see reality through the smoke and mirrors.

WHY LISTEN TO ME?

I wrote this book because I have become increasingly angry about the messages sent by the world of financial planners and others who sell financial products. I have come to the conclusion that most of them are simply wrong, and the strategies they ask us to follow can, in fact, suck the financial life out of us. I felt it was imperative to reveal what I believe to be the truth behind the myths we are asked to believe.

Those are my reasons for writing. But why should you read what I have to say?

First and most important, I am an independent source. I have no vested interest in your investments, or whether you have life insurance, or how large your RRSP is, because I don't sell any of those products.

Second, I have the education and experience necessary to explain what you need to know. I am a chartered accountant by profession and have provided financial services to many different types of businesses and individuals for more than 20 years. My training has given me the necessary tools to make some sense of the many complicated and confusing areas related to personal finances.

I have found that the skills I have developed and honed from years of creating and analyzing the financial statements of a diverse range of businesses translates well to the understanding of personal finances. In my own work and in this book, I have taken all the accounting concepts, principles, and procedures used in successful businesses and applied them to the finances of individuals.

WHO SHOULD READ THIS BOOK?

If you are independently wealthy, own your own mortgage-free home, have been able to maximize your RRSP contributions, have investments outside your retirement plan, spend less than you make each year, and are totally up-to-date on your personal income taxes, you won't get much out of this book.

It's for everyone else. If any of the following statements describes you, then you've picked up the right book:

- I know my personal finances need improvement but I just can't find the time to deal with them.
- I have a credit card balance that seems to go nowhere but up.
- I have no idea how well my investments are doing.
- I own a really nice house . . . with a really huge mortgage.

- I'm worried about my kids' education, but paying private school fees or saving for university is just adding to my financial pressure cooker.

- I own a whole life insurance policy, and the payments are killing me.

- I still owe personal income tax from prior years.

- I am a student or a recent university graduate with loans to pay off, and I haven't found a job yet.

- I have no idea how much I spent last year on interest.

- I am self-employed and behind on my personal taxes, GST, and payroll taxes.

- I never seem to be able to come up with the money to make my RRSP contribution unless I borrow it.

- I am not good with numbers.

If any item in this list describes you, don't despair. You're not alone. In fact, I would describe you as the typical Canadian — at least in terms of personal finances. But help is at hand. This book may become your best friend.

You may have noticed that the above list doesn't mention anything about income level. That's because earning a significant salary or income, even millions of dollars a year, doesn't necessarily mean you are in good shape financially. In fact, you may be in worse shape than someone with a much lower income, because your high income allows you to borrow easily. You can dig yourself into a very deep debt hole that will be extremely tough to get out of if your income is ever significantly reduced. If you fall into this camp, you too should benefit from the words that follow.

HOW THIS BOOK WILL HELP YOU

Reading this book and using the tools that come on the CD-ROM will give you what you need to take control of your personal finances, and that's something that most people never do. Many, if not most, people simply give up and assume that their money will "sort itself out in the end." Nothing could be further from the truth. If you don't take control, someone else will, and that could cost you and your family big time.

There are lots of reasons why so many Canadians have become dependent on the financial advice of the "experts" instead of controlling their own financial decision-making. Let's look at the three main reasons, and how the financial companies feed on them:

- *Lack of financial knowledge:* You may be very good at what you do — whether you are a plumber, a doctor, a professional athlete, or anything else — but you probably don't have much training in personal financial matters. If you're like most people, you've probably learned what you do know about finances from your parents, or perhaps from whatever reading you have done during your spare time. The financial companies, however, have thousands of employees trained in finance constantly working on developing products that will make them money. Many of these products are exceedingly complex and are designed in such a way that you may never be able to figure out whether or not they are good for you. Advantage: theirs.

- *Lack of time:* How much time did you spend tracking and analyzing your spending last year? When you last renewed your mortgage, how many hours did you spend researching alternatives? When that life insurance salesperson tried to sell you a whole life policy, did you have it analyzed by an independent professional? There simply aren't enough hours in the day to do all that's needed. Unfortunately, unless you set priorities to start devoting at least some time to your personal finances, one day it will be too late. Your income will stop but the bills won't. The financial companies know this, and make promises to save you precious time. But what have you saved if you don't understand the financial products you're buying? Advantage: theirs.

- *Not having the right tools:* Even if you do have the financial expertise as well as the time, you may not have the right tools to make an effective decision about your finances. For example, if you are trying to decide whether to lease or buy a car, you may have the figures, but do you know how to use a business calculator to determine which option is better? When you consider your mortgage options, can you produce an amortization schedule for each one to see which one will cost you the least in interest and allow you to pay off your debt the earliest? (Both these tools are explained in Part Two of this book.) Advantage: theirs.

The large financial institutions invest millions of dollars developing advertising campaigns designed to toy with our emotions and deftly pick our pockets as a result of our not having the knowledge, time, and tools to control our own finances. To sell insurance, they tempt us with early retirement thoughts; to make investments look attractive, they use seductive pictures such as a pristine cottage on a glassy lake or a luxury car. Who can resist?

This book will help you get on track toward controlling your own finances and resisting the siren call of the big financial companies.

WHAT'S BETWEEN THE COVERS?

This book is meant for you, the typical Canadian. It's not meant for the bankers, brokers, credit card companies, and certain financial planners and insurance agents. In fact, many of those people are not going to like what they read here, because it counters the advice they give to people every day. But for you, all the content in the following chapters is positive. It will give you the ammunition you need to fight back against the scare tactics and "rule of thumb" selling methods used to suck the money out of your pockets every day of your life.

The remaining chapters in Part One of this book expose the five key myths used by many financial advisers to secure their own financial futures by tricking you into giving them a pipeline to your hard-earned money:

- *Myth 1: If I had a $1,000,000. . . I could retire.* The myth that you need more than a million dollars to retire comfortably is a blatant attempt to grab more of your money without you even noticing. That's because the more money you hand over to your investment adviser, the more money he or she makes through commissions and other fees. In Chapter 2, I debunk this myth by using the ultimate weapon — personal financial tracking. I use a fictitious family, the Harts, to show you how to crunch real numbers to prove you need far less than many financial advisers would have you believe.

- *Myth 2: RRSPs are the Holy Grail of retirement.* While an RRSP plays an important part in achieving financial security, there is something far more important to address: how to deal with your debt (e.g., credit card balance, home mortgage, personal line of credit). In Chapter 3, I provide a no-risk strategy that will let you eliminate all your debt, including your mortgage, years before you retire.

- *Myth 3: Don't worry about your investments; you'll be fine in the long run.* The standard message for years has been to trust in the stock market because the average rate of return on stocks, in the long term, will be much better than that of fixed income products such as GICs (guaranteed investment certificates) and term deposits. But what many financial advisers don't reveal is the one simple figure you need: the personal rate of return you are making on your investment portfolio. And why don't they show you this figure? Because it's simply too hard for them to calculate, or because it would be too "confusing" to explain that your return was negative 10 percent last year? Maybe it's because they don't want you to know. In Chapter 4, you'll learn how to calculate your own personal rate of return on any investment portfolio using a simple spreadsheet that is included on the CD-ROM that comes with this book. All you need are the dates and amounts of money you invested and the current market value. You can take the results to your next meeting with your adviser and start having some useful discussions.

- *Myth 4: We have met the enemy, and he is the tax collector.* No one likes to pay taxes, and financial salespeople know it. But if you follow the advice many offer — to invest in a tax shelter, or to borrow to invest, for example — in order to lower your tax bill, you may end up broke. In Chapter 5, I use some real-life examples to prove my point: trying to avoid taxes often results in lousy financial decisions.

- *Myth 5: Secure your financial future: buy life insurance.* Let's face facts. Having a life insurance policy on your own life won't do anything to secure your financial future: you'll be dead if you collect. Life insurance does, however, serve a purpose. It should help your dependants maintain their standard of living after you are gone. But that's not what you'll hear from many insurance sales people. Instead you'll hear wonderful things about whole life insurance and how you can save money at the same time you insure your life! It's what they don't tell you that's dangerous to your financial well-being. Chapter 6 reveals the true cost of life insurance and includes step-by-step instructions to help you determine how much coverage you need.

I learned about these myths the hard way — by making the mistakes of following most of them. I exposed the myths by doing my own personal financial tracking. The experience I have gained in doing so is the basis of my opinions in Chapters 2 to 6. It is my hope that you can use my experience to help yourself in your own personal financial planning.

Part Two of this book will help you take the next step. It focuses on saving you thousands of dollars by showing you how to choose the right tools, understand mortgages (likely the largest investment you'll ever make), and describes in detail how to track your finances (the ultimate weapon in fighting back). Finally, it summarizes everything you'll have learned by that point and starts you in the right direction for the future.

What's on the CD-ROM?

The CD-ROM is an integral part of this book and provides valuable tools for you to use with your very own personal financial details. I encourage you to use these simple *Microsoft Excel* spreadsheets and arm yourself with the information only you can determine. Here's what you get:

- *The Personal Rate of Return Calculator:* Figure out what rate of return your RRSP has generated then look at the rate on your debt to figure out how much further ahead you'll be by paying off your loans.

- *The Retirement Optimizer:* Simply answer some basic questions to determine how much your RRSP will be worth when you want to retire, whether or not you can afford to retire early, how much retirement savings you will be forced to withdraw each year, and whether or not that will result in Old Age Security clawbacks, and much more.

- *My Net Worth Calculator:* Find out the most important figure in personal finances: the one that tells you what you are worth.

- *My Income and Expenses:* Punch in your monthly expenses and instantly see what your annual expenses are likely to be.

- *Cash Flow Projector:* If you have actual results, use this tool to allocate your spending and reach your goals.

After you've finished reading the book, why not keep in touch and continue learning? My website, <www.smoke-andmirrors.ca>, will regularly feature new content to keep you on top of your personal finances and will offer updated spreadsheets to readers of this book. Come for a visit and drop me a line about your own personal finances.

2

MYTH 1: IF I HAD A $1,000,000... I COULD RETIRE

EXPOSING THE MYTH

The Barenaked Ladies may not have been thinking about retirement when they wrote their popular song "If I Had $1,000,000," but they could have been, based on the myth perpetuated by the financial community that you will need 70 percent of your final pre-retirement income to maintain your standard of living after you retire. If that were true, it would mean that you would probably need to build up more than a million dollars in investments to earn the required income.

Most financial advisers perpetuate this myth because the more money you hand over to them, the more money they make through commissions and other fees. I have even heard some of them dismiss the Canada Pension Plan (CPP) and Old Age Security (OAS) pension out of hand, as if there is no chance of these plans surviving until you retire. "Better crank up your savings instead," they warn.

Can We Rely on the CPP and OAS Pensions?

First of all, the Canada Pension Plan is not run by the big financial institutions. The responsibility for its operation rests jointly with the federal and provincial ministers of finance. It is financed through mandatory contributions from employees, employers, and self-employed Canadians. The government sets the contribution rates and ensures that employees and employers pay their fair share through payroll taxes and, in the case of the self-employed, through personal income tax returns.

Canada's chief actuary is required to produce an actuarial report every three years to ensure that the plan will be able to fund existing and future retiring Canadians. The last report was in 2001, and it concluded that a 9.9 percent contribution rate should sustain it over the long term. The results were also reviewed by a team of independent actuaries, and they agreed with the conclusions.

To ensure the investments of the CPP are being handled effectively, the CPP Investment Board was created in 1997 to invest funds not required to pay current benefits. It operates at arm's length and carefully monitors the asset allocation and returns of the investments.

The March 31, 2002, audited financial statements of the CPP showed $51.7 billion in net assets. At March 31, 2003, that had risen to $53.7 billion. While not perfect, it sounds quite solid to me.

The Old Age Security pension is not based on employment earnings. It's paid out of current government tax revenues and begins at age 65. Can you imagine the election campaign of the next federal party that says they are going to get rid of the OAS pension? Right — it's not very likely.

The next time your advisor dismisses the CPP and OAS plans, review the facts and ask him or her exactly why he or she has more confidence in his or her own ability to take care of your retirement.

Myth versus Reality

Many people base their current financial goals on when they think they are going to retire and how much money they assume they will need. Everyone has a different retirement dream: some may want to continue working until they drop; others desire to be financially independent by age 55 and spend the rest of their days on the beach. Whatever your plan, you want to avoid the common financial traps that may ruin your dreams.

The *actual* amount of money you need to save depends less on this 70 percent formula and more on your spending habits, debt levels, and future investment rates of return; that is, the percentage by which your investments grow each year, and the rate they'll pay after you retire. The problem is that nobody can accurately predict what the future will bring. Will the Toronto Stock Exchange, for example, continue to earn about 8 percent a year, as it has over the last 50 years? And, of course, your rate of return will depend on which investments you choose to make.

Your Investment Options

When it comes to deciding where to invest your money, you have several basic options: equities (stocks), bonds, and fixed-income products (term deposits, GICs, etc.). Equities are the riskiest, and fixed-income products are the most secure. However, you will pay for security with lower rates of return. The upside is that you generally won't suffer from a decline in value with fixed-income products.

Judging Your Comfort Level

If you want to achieve a higher rate of return than that which fixed-income products can offer, you'll have to accept a greater degree of risk that your investments may decline in value. A lot of people learned that lesson during the "dot com" crash. Some people made incredible returns on their investments in the high-tech and dot-com stocks at first. In some cases, investments more than doubled overnight. But those returns came at a risk that was soon realized. There were many people who lost their entire investments when the market crashed.

If the thought of losing money makes your stomach churn, investing in the stock market may not be for you, no matter what your age. If that's your situation, don't invest in stocks. There's absolutely nothing wrong with that decision. Whatever you decide, you want to be able to sleep at night. Be prepared, however, for a lower rate of return.

Calculating a Realistic Rate of Return

With retirement planning, it's best to be conservative when choosing a rate of return. Assuming you will receive a 10 percent return may give you a warm feeling, but you will find yourself significantly short of retirement funds if actual results turn out to be much lower.

In this book, I have chosen to assume that the future may not be as rosy as the past, and that as you approach retirement, you will need to reduce your exposure to risk by switching to lower rate fixed-income investments. Therefore, in the examples in this book I use an average annual rate of return of 5 percent. When doing your own analysis, you should use a rate that reflects your own beliefs and attitudes toward risk tolerance.

DEBUNKING THE RULE OF 70 PERCENT

Consider this example: assume the year before you retire your combined household income is $100,000. The rule of thumb says you will need 70 percent of your pre-retirement income, or $70,000 per year during retirement to maintain your lifestyle. Assuming that you could earn an interest rate of 5 percent annually, you would need to build up investments of $1,400,000 ($1,400,000 x 5% = $70,000). With interest compounding at 5 percent, you would need to save $3,406 a month, or $40,872 a year, for 20 years to reach your goal. If you are at a higher income level, the news is worse. For example, if final household income is $120,000, then according to the rule of thumb, you would need 70 percent of that, or $84,000. To achieve that amount, you would need a total of $1,680,000 in investments earning 5 percent per year. To get there, you would need to save $4,087 per month, or $49,044 a year, for 20 years.

That kind of saving isn't reasonable for most people, but don't panic. Remember: it's just a myth.

First of all, you probably won't need 70 percent of your pre-retirement income after you retire because you won't have many of the expenses you had before, such as mortgage payments; childcare; schooling costs; children's food, clothing, and entertainment costs; car-lease payments; and vacation costs for a family, to name a few.

The best way to analyze what you'll actually need isn't to use a simple percentage, but to assess where your money is going right now. Then you'll be able to clearly see if there are expenses you can reduce, and you'll certainly see what expenses may not even exist in your retirement years. So step 1 is calculating your expenses for the last year (if you have not already done so). If you don't do this, the whole process will be at risk. Just as any successful business keeps accurate and current financial records, you too need good information about your past spending habits in order to plan for your future. (Later on, in Chapter 10, you'll learn all you need to know about how to set up and track your finances.)

Let's look at an example that shows why the 70 percent myth is just that, and to give you some ideas for your own retirement planning. Meet the Hart family, who will serve throughout this book as one family's trek to successful financial and retirement planning. Your own financial affairs, of course, will be different, but you can use the story of the Harts as a touchstone for making your sound financial decisions.

MEET THE HARTS TODAY

Joe and Karen Hart are both 42 years old. They have two children: Colin, age 6, and Anita, who is 3. They live in a detached house in the suburbs.

Life is hectic for the Harts. Joe works as a computer software designer for a small company, and Karen is an accounting supervisor in a large downtown law firm. Anita goes to a daycare downtown, and Colin is in grade 1 at a public school near the house. Each weekday means a lot of travel time, as Joe takes Colin to school and goes on to work, and Karen does the same with Anita.

Work life is also stressful. Joe's company is constantly on the hunt for venture capital, and there is a real possibility that he may lose his job if new investors can't be found.

Joe and Karen make a combined income of $100,000, but after deducts for income tax, Employment Insurance, and Canada Pension Plan, they're left with a net income of $38,546 each. That's $77,092 for the family to cover all their expenses.

The Harts lease two automobiles: a Ford Taurus and a Honda Accord. With two kids and two jobs, they need both cars. They bought their house several years ago for $275,000; the mortgage at the beginning of the current year was $200,000, so they still are making substantial payments on it.

Now let's look at where the rest of the money went. The following spending record summarizes their outflows (i.e., all expenses plus any debt repayments and investments) for the year:

Expenses	$
Automobiles (2 leased cars)	14,756
Cash expenses	3,300
Children (daycare, lessons, babysitter)	3,900
Clothing	4,000
Entertainment (movie rentals, gifts, vacations)	4,650
Groceries	7,550
House (mortgage interest, property tax)	15,250
Insurance (house, car, life)	3,100
Interest and bank charges (bank, credit card)	2,100
Medical	1,600
Restaurants	2,980
Utilities (gas/oil, hydro, cable TV)	4,300
Total Expenses	**67,486**
Debt Repayment, Investments	
House mortgage principal	5,384
RRSPS	8,000
Total Debt Repayment, Investments	**13,384**
Total Outflows	**80,870**

You will have noticed that the Harts' outflow of $80,870 is greater than the $77,092 they bring home each year. You may be wondering how this is possible. The Harts managed the same way many Canadians do: they used their credit cards and accumulated debt. In fact, they accumulated a debt of $5,048, charging 19 percent interest. On an annual basis, that will cost them $959 in interest — money that can never be recovered.

Of course, it is vital that the Harts get their spending under control before they entertain any thoughts of a comfortable retirement. They need to pay off their debts first; then they can start thinking about those years down the road. (Chapter 10 covers how to gain control over your expenses.)

THE HARTS AFTER RETIREMENT

Joe and Karen's situation will change considerably after they retire, and they know that their expenses will be reduced at that time. Here are the categories in which they expect to realize some savings:

- *Automobiles:* Joe and Karen probably won't need two cars, since they won't have two jobs to go to and won't be doing the "double kid shuffle." If they get rid of one of the cars — say the Honda — that will reduce their expenses by $6,885 per year, as that is what the leasing and operating costs came to last year. As for the other car, there will probably be a lot less mileage and wear, since there won't be daily trips to the office, school, and daycare. They could also consider buying instead of leasing their car. (From a financial point of view, owning a car is a much better idea, both before and after retirement.) A well-maintained car should last eight to ten years, and possibly even longer. In the Harts' case, the cars should be purchased before retirement to end the continual cash drain of leasing. Purchasing a car next time will eventually lead to payment-free years, reducing expenses of the main car by the leasing costs: $4,536 a year.

- *Cash expenses, children, clothing:* As with most families, a large portion of the cash in the Hart family is spent on the children. After retirement, those expenses will be gone because the kids will have grown up and left home. To be conservative, let's say only $1,000 of the $3,300 was spent on them. That's $1,000 less per year the couple will need after the kids move out. Direct children costs will also be eliminated, resulting in annual savings of $3,900. Clothing costs will also decline, let's say by $2,000 in this case.

- *Entertainment:* Let's assume entertainment expenses will not decline. With more free time the Harts expect to increase the number of movie rentals and vacations. The actual dollar amount will not increase, however, because the costs of the added rentals and trips will be lower than when they had to pay for the children travelling with them on vacation.

- *Groceries:* Grocery costs will also decline by an estimated $2,000 with half the number of mouths to feed.

- *House:* The current household mortgage is $200,000. It bears interest at 6 percent a year and is amortized over 20 years. The monthly payments are $1,424. After the mortgage has been eliminated, the Harts can cross off $17,092 from the outflows ($11,708 in interest and $5,384 in principal payments). Only the property taxes of $3,542 will remain.

- *Insurance:* Insurance costs should decline when the Harts cut back to using one car. They may also decide to cancel the life insurance as they age. However, to be conservative, they decide to leave the costs the same.

- *Interest and bank charges:* These should decline as Joe and Karen are determined to pay off their credit card debt of $5,048 and stay away from costly bank overdraft protection interest charges. After retirement, only minimal bank charges should remain. That's another expense reduction of about $1,500 a year.

- *Medical, restaurants, and utilities:* The Harts assume that the total of medical costs, restaurant meals, and utilities will not decline.

- RRSPS: Joe and Karen will no longer be making RRSP contributions after retirement, which will result in lower cash outflows of $8,000.

To sum up, after Joe and Karen retire, they will reduce their cash outflows by an astounding $46,913 to $33,957, less than half what they are spending now. Here's how today's expenses compare to post-retirement expenses:

Expenses	Current $	After Retirement $
Automobiles	14,756	3,335
Cash expenses	3,300	2,300
Children (daycare, lessons, babysitter)	3,900	0
Clothing	4,000	2,000
Entertainment (movie rentals, gifts, vacations)	4,650	4,650
Groceries	7,550	5,550
House (mortgage interest, property tax)	15,250	3,542
Insurance (house, car, life)	3,100	3,100
Interest and bank charges	2,100	600
Medical	1,600	1,600
Restaurants	2,980	2,980
Utilities (gas/oil, hydro, cable TV)	4,300	4,300
Total Expenses	**67,486**	**33,957**

Debt Repayment, Investments		
House mortgage principal	5,384	0
RRSPS	8,000	0
Total Debt Repayment, Investments	**13,384**	**0**
Total Outflows	**80,870**	**33,957**

This comparison of expenses reveals that the Harts will have to earn only approximately $40,000 per annum ($20,000 each) to net $33,957 after tax ($16,979 each) because they will both be in lower tax brackets and not have CPP and EI withheld after they retire. This amount is only 40 percent of their combined annual salary of $100,000 — far less than the 70 percent proposed by the myth supported by many financial advisers.

FROM MYTH TO REALITY

So if the 70 percent myth isn't true, then how do you calculate how much you will need and where you'll get the money?

First, consider that you will have other sources besides the interest on your RRSP investments. So far, the calculations we've made are based on the assumption that you will live off investment interest and keep the principal to pass on to your children or other beneficiaries, which, perhaps, may be something you don't want — or need — to do. As you get older, you may feel comfortable relying on some of that principal for your daily expenses.

But even if you want to leave a significant portion of your RRSP investments intact, there are other sources of retirement income. These include the following:

- *Private pension plan:* If you've been one of the fortunate Canadians to have worked in a job that provides pension income, you will be able to rely on those payments.

- *Old Age Security (OAS):* The OAS pension is available to Canadian citizens and legal residents of Canada aged 65 and older who have lived in Canada for at least ten years since turning 18 years of age. As of July 2004, the maximum monthly OAS benefit was $466.63 ($5,600 yearly). If your individual net income is more than $59,790, you must repay part of your OAS pension. The repayment amounts are normally deducted from your monthly payments before they are issued. The full OAS pension is eliminated if your net income is $96,972 or more.

- *Canadian Pension Plan (CPP):* If you pay into CPP during your working life, you are eligible for pension benefits as early as age 60. The maximum monthly CPP benefit payable for those at least 65 years old in 2004 was $814.17 per month or $9,770 annually.

Keep in mind that both OAS and CPP are adjusted for inflation. CPP is adjusted annually in January, and OAS is adjusted quarterly. These adjustments will, to a large degree, offset rising expenses. (For current rates for OAS and CPP, check out the website <http://www.sdc.gc.ca/en/gateways/nav/top_nav/program/isp.shtml>.)

Now you can breathe a little easier knowing that you don't need 70 percent of your income for your retirement years. That is likely a relief — but you still need to determine what you *will* need. Let's revisit the Harts to see how their calculations are coming along.

THE HARTS: MAKING THE CALCULATIONS

Joe and Karen have determined that they will need $40,000 per year in their retirement years. If they want to live solely off investment income, they will need to build up their investments to about $800,000, if they assume they can earn a 5 percent return ($800,000 x 5% = $40,000). That's a daunting figure for a couple who are already in debt and living a busy, stressful life.

But here Joe and Karen need to stop and consider other sources of income. First, they will also have available to them the money they have invested over all the years in their RRSPs. According to the tax rules, their RRSPs must be converted to a registered retirement income fund (RRIF) or annuity before December 31 of the year in which they turn 69. They then must begin withdrawing from their RRIFs at set rates each year. The minimum required withdrawal is a percentage based on the market value of the assets in the plan at the start of each year, ranging from 5 percent at age 70 up to 20 percent at age 94. Of course, Joe and Karen are free to do what they want with the money they withdraw, and they could reinvest it in another type of financial product, although it won't be sheltered from tax as it was when it was in the RRSPs. (More about RRIFs in Chapter 3.)

If they want to count on the RRIF funds for daily living expenses, Joe and Karen would need to have built up an RRSP worth $563,800 at retirement to generate annual RRIF payouts of $40,000 (at 5 percent for 25 years until they are 90 years old). The total, $563,800, is a lot less daunting to them than $800,000, the figure they started with, but it's still quite a bit of money.

The combined value of the couple's RRSPs are currently only $60,000. To build that up to $563,800 by age 65 (23 years) they would need to save $9,160 a year at a rate of return of 5 percent per annum, which is more than what they are investing in RRSPs right now.

But there is more good news. Both Joe and Karen will be eligible for OAS when they turn 65, and they will not have to repay any of it, since their net incomes will be well below the "clawback" level. This means they can count on receiving $5,600 each, or $11,200, from the government every year. That reduces the amount that they will have to finance themselves from $40,000 to $28,800.

As well, because they both have paid into CPP all their working lives, they will be able to depend on those pension payments too. They determine that they will be eligible to receive the maximum monthly CPP benefit ($9,770 x 2 = $19,540), which will again reduce the amount they need to finance themselves. Now they need to find a way to come up with only $9,260 a year more.

The result: Joe and Karen now realize that they have to build up their RRSPs to a value of $130,510 by age 65 to provide $9,260 per year for 25 retirement years, assuming a 5 percent rate of return. The $60,000 they have already will rise to $184,300 in 23 years if the investments earn an average of 5 percent per year. They could reach their goal without even contributing any more money!

Things don't look so daunting now compared to their initial calculation, when they believed the 70 percent myth, which told them they would need $1,400,000. With their existing RRSPs rising to $184,300, they thought they needed another $1,215,700 to reach their goal, requiring them to save $29,343 per year for 23 years at 5 percent. Is it any wonder Joe and Karen used to get depressed after a visit to their investment adviser?

THE NET WORTH STATEMENT

It's time to look at something that most people never see but which is the most vital piece of information in the quest for a financially secure retirement: the net worth statement. How it looks when you retire will determine how comfortable your twilight years will be.

Your personal net worth statement is like a company's balance sheet. It shows the current value of all assets owned and liabilities owed at a point in time. It is different than your spending record, which is similar to a company's income statement and shows what amount of money came in and where it went over a period of time (usually a year).

After you stop working you won't have any employment income to pay your expenses. Unless you are scheduled for a great inheritance or win the lottery, the assets on your net worth statement at that time will be all that brings in money to pay your expenses (besides government and other pensions).

For most people, a house is their biggest asset. Owning a home is an excellent investment, especially if the mortgage is paid off. You have several options that can help you significantly. You could sell the home outright, pocket the proceeds tax-free, and buy a smaller house or a condominium. You could even move into a rental unit and make payments on a monthly basis. Alternatively, you could take out an equity line of credit. Any of these options would free up a significant amount of cash to handle emergencies or changes in circumstances. However, you also must be aware that you'll be eating into your net worth by adding debt, and that might not be too popular with your kids!

The debts (liabilities) are just as important as your assets when you retire. Your cash outflows are going to be a lot higher if you still have debts. You'll need to have saved a lot more money before retirement to continue to make those payments.

Simply stated, your objective should be to maximize the value of your assets and eliminate all debts by the time you retire. If you have a current statement of net worth looking you in the face every year, it'll be much easier to ensure you are on the right track to making it the best it can be by the time you retire.

Now let's consider Joe and Karen's statement of net worth.

THE HARTS' NET WORTH

Here is Joe and Karen Hart's statement of net worth at the end of this year, compared to the end of last year:

Assets	31 Dec $ (last year)	31 Dec $ (this year)
Cash in bank	714	1,984
House (principal residence)	275,000	275,000
RRSP: Joe (market value)	36,900	40,000
RRSP: Karen (market value)	16,875	20,000
Total Assets	**329,489**	**336,984**
Liabilities		
Household mortgage	200,000	194,616
Credit card balance	0	5,048
Total Liabilities	**200,000**	**199,664**
Net Worth (Assets – Liabilities)	**129,489**	**137,320**

As you can see, they are in pretty good financial shape with a net worth of $137,320, which is better than last year by $7,831.

Even though they invested $8,000 in RRSPs this year and paid down the principal on their mortgage by $5,384, their net worth did not increase by the total of that investment plus debt principal repayments ($13,384). Why not? There are several reasons.

First of all, their RRSPs did not do so well, rising by only $6,225 ($60,000 – $53,775) even though they contributed $8,000. They in fact had a return this past year of –2.93 percent.

Second, as already mentioned, they spent $3,778 more than they made in the current year. The effect of their overspending has a significant effect on their net worth statement. At the end of last year, they had $714 in the bank and no credit card debt. At the end of this year, they had $1,984 in the bank but owed $5,048 on the credit card. They went from $714 in the bank to a net amount owing of $3,064 ($1,984 cash less $5,048 debt), a reduction of $3,778 — the exact amount by which they overspent.

If Joe and Karen pay off their credit card balance and get back to putting $8,000 per year into their RRSPs, their combined value will grow to $515,700 in 23 years at 5 percent. That's $376,300 more than the $139,400 minimum they have determined they would need. That amount will go a long way to covering many of the uncertainties they will face.

You may notice that there are some things missing from the net worth statement. Joe and Karen own personal property, including furniture, clothing, and electronic equipment, that is not listed. These types of items, while they have value, do not really contribute to the couple's ability to retire. This exercise is meant to analyze the couple's net worth with the objective of maximizing the amount of money they have and optimizing its structure to ensure that they can reach their retirement goals.

THE EFFECTS OF INFLATION

You'll note that I have used the Harts' current salaries and expenses and have not attempted to project them to final pre-retirement levels. This is done to keep the example simple. As time goes by, it's important to continually update your own figures, since even small changes can have significant effects on the future. We'll get into this in detail in Chapter 3.

Inflation will surely have an effect. In the case of the Harts, if inflation averages say, 3 percent a year until they retire in 23 years, their $100,000 combined salaries would rise to $197,360. Expenses will, of course, increase as well, but when those expenses are significantly reduced, so is the exposure to inflation.

The most common measure of inflation is the Consumer Price Index (CPI), which is the rate at which the price of a specific basket of goods rises each year. Because it is an average, it can be misleading. What is important to each of us is not some average figure, but the price of only what we buy as individuals. For example, if housing prices rise rapidly after you retire, it will only affect your expenses to the extent that your property taxes increase if they are based on market value. The inflationary effect on your house value would be a good thing, since usually you are in the market to sell rather than buy.

The Harts' current expenses are $67,486. If inflation averages 3 percent over the next 23 years, they will go up to $133,190. But after retirement, the Harts calculate their expenses will be only $33,957 in today's dollars. In 23 years that figure will rise to only $67,017 assuming 3 percent inflation. At the same time, their salaries will have increased by $97,360 due to inflation, so inflation actually works in the Harts' favour. If the examples used in this chapter for the Harts were adjusted for inflation, you would see that the couple would be even better off.

SUMMARY

However much you will need in retirement, it should be clear by now that it probably *won't* be 70 percent of your income. In the case of the Harts, they've learned that they could get by on less than half of the money they make now and that they could get there without contributing anything more to their RRSPs. Your case will most certainly be different. You may need more or maybe less.

If you have done your own calculations and determined that you'll only need half of what you make now, does that mean you no longer need to invest or be concerned about your future? Of course not. After you pay off all your debts, you want to put away as much as you can for the future as a cushion against events such as rising medical expenses or simply as a supplement to your travel fund.

Read on to learn more ways to do so — ways that are probably not in accordance with what you've heard from your financial adviser.

3

MYTH 2: RRSPs ARE THE HOLY GRAIL OF RETIREMENT

EXPOSING THE MYTH

If you are like most Canadians, when someone asks you about your retirement plans, you probably start talking about your registered retirement savings plan (RRSP). That's because most Canadians don't have a gold-plated company pension plan to rely on.

But RRSPs are *not* the Holy Grail of retirement planning, and you want to be careful before jumping into the yearly sales pitches that pressure you to invest the maximum allowed. This doesn't mean RRSPs should be avoided. Used wisely, they can be a significant part of a secure retirement. The problem is that most people focus only on their RRSPs and forget the other parts that are even more important — their spending patterns and debt levels.

The real benefit of an RRSP is that it allows you to delay paying taxes until you withdraw the money. That's a real economic gain because of the time value of money — you can use the tax refund now and have to pay it back only when you retire. If your RRSP investments rise, they can produce a great nest egg and save you money in the process. And that's why I do recommend that you start investing in RRSPs effectively — but *only* after you pay off all your personal debt, including your house mortgage.

THE WARM BATH

Think about retirement as a nice warm bath. You're busting your buns your whole working life to fill that bathtub with soothing hot water so you can soak your aching bones after work. But what's the most efficient way to do it? Most people get advice on how to fill their bathtub from a bathwater salesperson. What is this person going to tell you? They'll most likely look into your tub and give a thoughtful "Hmmm . . ." and say, "Gee, there's not much water in there. You should have started filling it much earlier. You're going to have to put a lot more in from now on if you want to have any hope of filling this bathtub! Oh, and by the way, we can help you."

But there's something important that the salesperson hasn't told you and that you haven't noticed — the plug is missing! That's right: water — and in the case of personal finances, money — is flowing down the drain every second of every day as you are trying to fill up your tub.

Here's the key: put the plug in and then start filling!

Let's bring the analogy back to finances. Have you ever heard a similar pitch from a mutual fund salesperson? Don't listen. Instead, take control.

AN RRSP PRIMER

Let's review the basics before discussing when and how you should begin investing more of your hard-earned money in an RRSP. (We'll deal extensively with how much to put in your RRSP in Chapter 7.)

An RRSP is not simply an investment. It is a government-sanctioned registered program that allows you to save for your retirement. You are allowed to invest in a broad range of products within an RRSP, including GICs, mutual funds, individual stocks, and bonds. There are strict rules on how much you are allowed to invest and the portion that must be Canadian.

RRSP Limits

Your RRSP limit for the current year is determined as follows:

- Your unused RRSP deduction limit carried forward from prior years

- Plus 18 percent of your previous year's earned income (up to a maximum of $15,500 in 2004, $16,500 in 2005, and $18,000 for 2006)

- Less any pension adjustment for the prior year (for those who have company pension plans)

(**Note:** Earned income includes salary, wages, and self-employment income but not investment income.)

Foreign Content

You are currently allowed to hold up to 30 percent of your RRSP in foreign investments based on their "book value" (i.e., the cost of the investment plus any mutual fund distributions). For example, if you invest $10,000 in your RRSP and put $7,000 in a Canadian GIC, you could invest up to $3,000 in a foreign mutual find. Even if the foreign investment rises in value to, say, $4,000, and your Canadian content stays at $7,000, you are still all right. That is why your RRSP statement shows you the book value — to make sure you stay within the foreign content limits.

Timing

For an RRSP contribution to be deductible, it must be made within 60 days of the calendar year-end (i.e., March 1, or February 29 in a leap year). If the deadline falls on a weekend, it is extended to the next business day.

DEBUNKING THE PROMISES OF RRSPs

The mythology of the power of RRSPs is really an accumulation of several claims that have built up over time. Let's look at each in turn.

Start Yesterday

Here's the claim: If you want to retire in comfort, you have to put money into your RRSP every year, and it's best to start when you are young. The younger the better. If you start an RRSP when you are just 22 years old and you put $4,000 in per year until you are 65 at an annual rate of return of 8 percent, your RRSP will be worth $1.3 million when you retire!

I am tired of hearing this pitch because it's really nothing more than a slick marketing trick that can be lethal to your financial health. There are many problems with it.

First, consider who is sending the message. It's all the usual suspects: banks, brokerage houses, and most "financial advisers." Why do they want you to fall for this message? Because for every dollar you put in, they get a percentage. It's a guaranteed annuity for them, regardless of what happens to your investments along the way.

When you hand over your money to your adviser or banker to invest in an RRSP, he or she will do as you ask and invest it for you. If he or she invests in a mutual fund, in addition to any upfront commission, he or she will also get a fee from the mutual fund company. You will never know how much your adviser or banker is getting, however, because this cost is buried in the expenses of the mutual fund company. This cost is included in the management expense ratio, or MER. It represents the ratio of costs, including commissions and marketing expenses, as a percentage of the total assets of the mutual fund. All investors in that fund are paying those management expenses, and it can all add up to a lot of money.

For example, say the managers of the mutual fund were able to realize a return on their investments of 7 percent. If the MER is 2 percent, the overall rate of return on that mutual fund would be only the net amount of 5 percent. The theory is that the managers are being rewarded for generating above-average returns. That's fine if they do indeed generate that kind of return, but in many cases they don't. Your broker and the mutual fund company win. You lose.

The second problem with this claim is that it ignores some basic facts of life. Where is the typical 22-year-old going to come up with $4,000 per year? He or she has possibly just graduated from university and perhaps has a student loan. As with any debt, that loan will have a fixed interest rate that in many cases will exceed what can be earned in the RRSP. (See Chapter 4 for more information.) Nor should a 22-year-old borrow the money to invest in an RRSP. Increasing debt at this age is the last thing anyone should be considering. No one is even *allowed* to invest in an RRSP until he or she has a job or other earned income to create RRSP contribution room.

Lastly, does it make sense for a 22-year-old to be worried about retirement? In every stage of life, you need to set your priorities both personally and financially. What about seeing the world and enjoying some life experiences before settling down to marriage, kids, a home, and all the rest? Frankly, I don't think focusing on retirement from the day he or she gets out of school is the best advice to give a young adult!

Borrow If You Don't Have the Funds

"Don't have the cash for an RRSP contribution? No problem. We'll lend you the money!"

You can hear that offer every February. Here's why you shouldn't listen to it.

Borrowing to invest makes sense in the long term only if the rate of return exceeds the interest rate on the loan. Obviously, it doesn't make sense to borrow at 5 percent to invest in a term deposit making only 2 percent! If you do borrow to invest, you are essentially agreeing to put all your eggs in one basket — the stock market — and hoping that it beats the rate on your loan. Once again, this strategy plays directly into the hands of those people who make a living off your finances.

Invest in an RRSP before Paying Down the Mortgage

This question of whether or not it's wise to invest in an RRSP before paying off the mortgage also comes up every year. The usual answer is that you should contribute the maximum to your RRSP and use the tax refund to pay down your mortgage. Sounds like a good compromise doesn't it? This way, the finance company gets your investment money and it's up to you to be disciplined enough to actually use the refund to pay down your mortgage. Of course, that's easier said than done.

First of all, you need to be able to afford to pay down your mortgage. In other words you mustn't need the refund for anything else, such as paying down other debt or taking a much-needed vacation. Second, usually you can only pay down a mortgage when the finance company allows you to. Often that's only once a year and is limited to 15 percent to 20 percent of the outstanding balance. You have to be very disciplined and make sure you put the refund into a safe place until then.

The reality is that investing in an RRSP and using the tax refund to pay down the mortgage is usually not a compromise at all. The people who send this message are, in fact, simply wanting you to invest in an RRSP. Period. I am saying pay down the mortgage instead. Period.

Another Problem with RRSPs

What happens if you are heavily invested in stocks when you are about to retire? What about the thousands of other baby boomers in the same situation? Lots of Canadians are going to be forced to sell their stocks and mutual funds to fund their retirements. Some will start earlier, and some will be able to afford to delay withdrawing money until age 70, when they must begin making the minimum RRIF withdrawals. What will that do to the stock market? No one knows for sure, but if more people are selling than buying, it's most likely direction is down.

This will be happening at the worst time possible — when there is no time left to correct it and when no employment income can be earned to replace it. You may want to consider reducing your exposure to this risk, and that means reducing your investments in stocks and equity mutual funds.

ANOTHER DAY OLDER AND DEEPER IN DEBT?

If you focus all your resources and efforts on your RRSP and not on eliminating your debts, you'll probably still be left with those mortgage payments, car loan, or lease payments, and maybe even credit card balances when you retire. I have said it before, but it bears repeating: you will need to save a lot more money for retirement if you have to continue making all those payments.

From the bank or finance company's point of view, of course, your being in debt at retirement is ideal. Think about it. They get commissions and fees on all your RRSP contributions from the time you start to invest until you retire. They lock you into as much debt as possible: a mortgage, car loans or lease payments, credit card debt, and perhaps a home equity line of credit for good measure. You continue paying them even after you retire. That way, they'll also "work the spread" and make money off the deposits from other people who are funding your loans. They are winning on both sides of the balance sheet — investments from you and loans to you — who is losing? You guessed it: you are.

Debt: The Good, the Bad, and the Ugly

In Canada today, only the fortunate few can afford to pay cash for big-ticket items such as houses and cars. The rest of us must finance these purchases or we'd never get to own them. Mortgages and car loans are examples of good debt. It is necessary for us to take on this kind of debt to begin enjoying the assets, with an added bonus for houses — the value of that particular asset generally increases over time. The other advantage is one of cash flow. After the house and car are paid off, you will require less cash to live each year, and that ties into the idea of optimizing your RRSP, as we'll soon discuss.

Bad debt, however, includes lines of credit used to finance things such as vacations and luxury items like TVs and electronic gadgets. While the things we purchase this way may make us feel good, they are coming at a price — interest. Waiting until you have earned the cash to buy the things will save you a lot.

Ugly debt? Think credit cards and interest on personal income taxes owing from prior years.

AN ALTERNATIVE STRATEGY

Now for a radical thought. If paying off all personal debt before you retire is a good idea, why not focus on paying it all off even sooner? Why not forget RRSP contributions altogether until you pay off all debt, including your house mortgage?

Consider the rate of return on your debt with this strategy. For example, suppose you have a house mortgage at 6 percent, a car loan at 8 percent, and a credit card balance at 19 percent. Simply by paying off your debts instead of investing in an RRSP, you can realize a guaranteed after-tax return of between 6 percent and 19 percent, and there is no risk related to this rate of return.

Now let's consider this strategy in the case of Joe and Karen Hart.

THE HARTS: INVESTING IN RRSPs VERSUS PAYING DOWN THE DEBT

If Joe and Karen continue to spend more than they make, any financial strategy will almost certainly be doomed to failure. But they are determined to get their spending under control, and want to know, therefore, whether they will do better by investing $8,000 a year ($4,000 each) in RRSPS (see Chart 1: RRSP Option) or paying down their mortgage by $8,000 a year (see Chart 2: Mortgage Pay-Down Option).

They begin their calculations as of December 31 of last year, when they had no credit card debt, and make the following assumptions:

- The RRSPs will grow at an average rate of 5 percent per year.
- The mortgage rate will remain at 6 percent annually.
- Their marginal personal tax rates are 31 percent.
- The tax savings on the RRSP contributions will be reinvested in those RRSPS (i.e., they have sufficient contribution room).

Note that we will only look at the effect on net worth of two lines on the Harts' net worth statement: total RRSP value and mortgage balance. We are assuming the other lines (cash in bank, house value, etc.) will be the same for both scenarios. Here is a comparison of the two scenarios after 1, 5, 11, and 20 years:

CHART 1
RRSP OPTION

$8,000 RRSP CONTRIBUTIONS	31-Dec Last Year	31-Dec Year 1	31-Dec Year 5	31-Dec Year 11	31-Dec Year 20
ASSETS RRSPs (Combined)	$53,775	$66,956	$126,607	$241,031	$489,609
LIABILITIES Household mortgage	$200,000	$194,660	$169,799	$119,348	$0
NET WORTH EFFECT (Assets – liabilities)	-$146,225	-$127,704	-$43,192	$121,683	$489,609

CHART 2
MORTGAGE PAY-DOWN OPTION

$8,000 TO MORTGAGE	31-Dec Last Year	31-Dec Year 1	31-Dec Year 5	31-Dec Year 11	31-Dec Year 20
ASSETS RRSPs Combined)	$53,775	$56,464	$68,632	$91,974	$507,025
LIABILITIES Household mortgage	$200,000	$186,437	$123,286	$0	$0
NET WORTH EFFECT (Assets – liabilities)	-$146,225	-$129,973	-$54,654	$91,974	$507,025

The results after one year are very close. The RRSP option shows -$127,704, while the mortgage pay-down option shows a -$129,973 effect on net worth. Even after five years, the RRSP option beats the mortgage pay-down option by $11,462 (the difference between -$43,192 and -$54,654).

After 11 years, the RRSP option is still ahead by $29,709 ($121,683 less $91,974), but there is an important factor to consider — income tax.

The RRSP option shows a higher RRSP value, but to access those funds, the Harts would have to pay taxes on any withdrawal. To pay off the mortgage, they would have to cash in $196,000 of their RRSPs to be left with the required $119,348. That's $98,000 from each RRSP, less the $38,326 in tax they each would have to pay if it was added to their $50,000 salaries. They would be left with the required $59,674 each ($119,348 in total). That would leave them with only $45,031 in RRSPs, versus $91,974 for the mortgage pay-down scenario. The higher amount of net worth is deceptive because a large portion of it is pre-tax.

With the debt pay-down strategy, the Harts' mortgage will be paid off in 11 years (in fact, in ten years and seven months). That will leave them with more than nine mortgage-free years. During those last nine years, they will have an extra $1,424 per month to invest. That's the money that will no longer be going to the mortgage, and it adds up to more than $17,000 a year. Now they can begin to focus on their RRSPs in earnest.

After 20 years, the debt pay-down scenario shows a net worth slightly higher than for the RRSP scenario — a difference of $17,416 ($507,025 less $489,609). So after 20 years, the Harts would arrive at a similar point but would have taken a very different journey. The debt pay-down scenario, however, has two major advantages: it reduces the risk that the Harts could lose their house during the nine years of mortgage-free living, and there is less risk related to investment returns. (How much confidence do you have that the markets are going to post better returns than the interest rate on your debt? Are you willing to stake your family's future on it?)

THE BURDEN OF DEBT

Think of debt as a ball and chain attached to your ankle. That's what is holding you back in the race for financial freedom — not the fact that you didn't start contributing to an RRSP when you were a kid or that you haven't been able to max out your contributions.

In looking at the continuing story of the Harts, we see a family that is in good financial shape. The only debt they have is their mortgage. But what about people who aren't in such a strong financial position? If the debt pay-down option beats the RRSP when dealing with only a mortgage at 6 percent, think about those people with credit card debt at 19 percent or higher.

Credit Card Debt

Credit card debt is probably the most common debt for many Canadians. Anyone with credit card debt should pay it off first before making another RRSP contribution. You simply can't beat the rate of return. Let's look at an example.

Billy has $10,000 owing on his super-deluxe gold credit card. He is being charged 19 percent a year for his past indulgences. He is in the 40 percent tax bracket and therefore would receive a 40 percent tax refund on an RRSP contribution. He also has an extra $300 per month available.

This is what Billy discovers when he runs the figures through a simple spreadsheet program to compare paying down debt to making RRSP contributions:

- Billy would have to make monthly payments of $259.41 to pay off his credit card in five years (60 months). If he puts his $300 per month plus his tax savings into an RRSP, he will have paid off the credit card and have a balance of $28,358 in his RRSP at the end of five years.

- If instead of putting the $300 a month into an RRSP, Billy adds it to his regular credit card payments, he would have the debt cleared in just over 21 months. He could then start investing $559.41 a month in his RRSP (the $259.41 he would still be paying under the RRSP option plus the $300). At the end of five years, his RRSP would be worth $32,699. That's $4,341 better off.

It bears repeating: pay off credit card debt first!

Income Tax Debt

If you owe personal taxes from prior years, the debt is attracting interest at the "prescribed rate" set by the government (6 percent, in the third quarter of 2004), and it's not tax deductible.

Tax debt isn't like credit card debt, which you can take decades to pay off, if you wish. The government wants its money and it wants it soon. They also have the power to collect the money by contacting your bank directly and demanding payment, freezing your bank account, garnishing your wages, possessing your assets, etc. In short, it can get ugly.

If you have this kind of debt, you don't want it hanging around. If you owe on your taxes, focus on paying that first — even before credit card debt.

THE JOYS OF DEBT-FREE LIVING

Stop for a minute and think about what it would be like not to have any debt at all — no credit card debt, nothing owing on the car, not even mortgage payments. There would be no pressure to bring in a salary to make the payments. If you were to lose your job or become disabled and lose your ability to work, you wouldn't be in danger of losing your house.

Free Disability Insurance

Paying off the mortgage is like providing your own disability or income protection insurance, and it is generally far more attractive than investing heavily in RRSPs.

It is generally accepted that the odds of becoming disabled are much higher than the odds of dying, yet many people are more likely to have life insurance than disability insurance. The costs associated with becoming disabled are also very high: not only will you have regular living costs, there also may be the costs of ongoing attendant care, medicine, and other charges. If you can't continue to earn income, you could be in trouble. If your house is paid for, your worries will be significantly reduced.

Using Your House for Emergency Funds

You may have heard of the rule of thumb that you should save up about three months of expenses, just in case you need extra money in times of an emergency. But if you've been trying to pay off debt and invest in RRSPs, where is that money going to come from?

At first glance, you might think that your RRSPs would provide a large fund to draw on in times of emergency. But you must remember: an RRSP is designed as a long-term savings vehicle, *not* as a temporary emergency fund. Here's why:

- First, if you withdraw funds from your RRSP, you will have to pay income tax on the withdrawal, which can be significant, depending on when the emergency funds need to be tapped. The amount withdrawn will be taxed based on your income level and in which province you live. If you withdraw $10,000 out of an RRSP, and you're taxed at 37 percent, for example, you'll receive only $6,300.

- Second, if you need to access your RRSP funds at a time when your investments are down in the stock market, you will be forced to realize your paper losses. If you have invested $10,000 in RRSPs, but the stock market has declined, your $10,000 may be worth only, say, $8,000 when you need to access it. If you need the funds, you'll have to sell them at $8,000, eliminating any hope that they could rise in value again in the future.

- Finally, if your RRSPs are invested in mutual funds, you need to consider the deferred fees. In many cases, mutual funds are purchased and no commission is paid unless they are cashed in before a certain time, often five years or longer. If you cash them in early, you will be penalized.

With the debt pay-down strategy, you may not have an emergency fund, but you will have something just as good — an equity interest in your house. That means if you find yourself needing money, you could tap into that equity and take out a secured line of credit. If your finances are in order, a credit check won't be a problem for you. In fact, if you pay everything off, there won't be any credit to check!

A WORD ABOUT RESPs AND GROUP RRSPs

Registered Education Savings Plans (RESPs) allow you to invest money to pay for a child's post-secondary education.

The contributions are not tax-deductible, but the investment income is allowed to grow in the plan on a tax-deferred basis. When the money is withdrawn to pay the tuition fees, the original contribution is returned tax free (since the original contributions were not deducted) and any income earned in the plan is generally taxed in the hands of the child that attends the post-secondary school.

The annual contribution limit allowed is currently $4,000 per beneficiary, up to a lifetime limit is $42,000. What makes RESPs so attractive, however, is the Canada Education Savings Grant (CESG). Under this plan, the federal government provides grants of up to 20 percent of annual contributions made to RESPs for beneficiaries up to and including age 17, to a maximum grant of $400 per year per beneficiary. For example, if you put $2,000 into an RESP for your child, the government will pay a grant of $400 to the RESP. That's like getting an immediate 20 percent return on your investment, and rivals the rate on many credit cards. If you decide to put money into an RESP instead of paying down debt, it's vital that you carefully monitor the fees and rate of return that the RESP is generating. (For more information on RESPs and CESGs go to <http://www.sdc.gc.ca /en/home.shtml>).

Another possible exception to the debt pay-down strategy is group RRSPs. Some employers who don't have a traditional company pension plan offer this type of saving vehicle: they match, up to a certain maximum, any RRSP contribution that the employee makes. Say they allow you to contribute 3 percent of your salary of $50,000. That's $1,500 from you and they match it with another $1,500 to your plan. The 3 percent is free money that's difficult to turn down, but you must remember to keep a close eye on the plan to make sure the returns are adequate and the fees are reasonable.

SUMMARY

Add up your monthly debt payments now. Think about what it would be like not to have to make any of those payments. You'd have a lot left each month to invest, and you'd have no risk of losing your house, your car, or getting in over your head on credit cards if you lost your job. Since you wouldn't owe anything to anyone, there would be no one who could take things away from you.

Think about the effect of paying down debt on your net worth. A reduction in your debt is the same as an increase in your assets. In fact, a reduction in personal debt is better than an increase in an RRSP, because to get at the RRSP, you would need to pay tax on the withdrawal. The value of your RRSP when you retire is only one line on your net worth statement. What's on the other lines can be far more significant in determining your level of comfort.

The key to planning for a stress-free, enjoyable retirement can be summed up simply: Pay off all your personal debt first, and then begin investing in RRSPs.

4

MYTH 3: DON'T WORRY ABOUT YOUR INVESTMENTS; YOU'LL BE FINE IN THE LONG RUN

EXPOSING THE MYTH

For many years, the mantra of the financial community has been that if you want to have any hope of retiring in good shape, it is imperative to put your trust in the stock market. Don't worry about the conflict of interest between the analysts and the investment bankers that work for the same brokerage firm. Put your trust in the CEOs running the big companies — they're working hard for you and wouldn't put their own agenda ahead of shareholders like you. The stock market will recover: it always has in the past. Don't miss out!

Is investing in the stock market really the way to go? I, for one, am no longer convinced. Let's look at some of the factors to consider.

Rate of Return versus Lending Rates

The past won't predict the future, but at least it's a starting point. Let's look at how the Toronto Stock Exchange (TSX) has done over the last 20 years.

The closing value of the S&P/TSX composite index in August 1984 was 2,388, and in July 2004 it was 8,398. During those 20 years, the average annual rate of return was 6.5 percent. That's not bad but it isn't great. During the last ten years, the index rose from 4,350 in August 1994 to 8,398 in July 2004. That's an annual rate of return of only 6.8 percent.

Meanwhile, the average chartered bank prime lending rate since 1994 has been 6.02 percent. That means that even if you had borrowed to invest and you matched the diversified performance of the TSX in your investment earnings, you would not be much further ahead. Factor in a few fees and you would have lost money.

Remember also that the measure of the market as a whole probably doesn't reflect your specific portfolio. To duplicate it, you would have to be 100 percent invested in equities — a risky proposition even for young people.

How Mutual Funds Eat Your Money

Most Canadians invest in mutual funds to try to tap into potentially good stock market returns. They sure sound like a great idea. You get professional money managers to make sure you are adequately diversified, and they charge only a nominal fee. Mutual funds use to work well when returns were good, but what's happened lately? With lower returns available in the stock market, most mutual funds haven't been doing too well for us. Unluckily for the mutual fund managers, that has put a spotlight on the fees they are charging us. Guess what? They aren't so nominal.

Let's look at how many of them drain away our money, without us even realizing it. Most Canadians don't want to pay an up-front commission to the broker, so they select a "deferred sales charge" (DSC) mutual fund. You don't pay a commission up front, but what does it really cost you? It costs you about 2.5 percent per year on average through the management expense ratio, including an annual "trailer fee" of somewhere around 0.5 percent every year you leave the money in the mutual fund, as I mentioned in the previous chapter. But there is another charge lurking.

The other, more significant fee is the cost to sell the mutual fund. With a DSC mutual fund, the penalty for not paying an up-front commission is that you are locked in for about six to eight years! What if the fund doesn't perform well, and you want to sell it? You'll pay a commission as high as 6 percent in the first year. That commission declines each year but doesn't reach zero until the locked-in period expires.

Why doesn't everyone just buy stocks then? Because putting all your eggs in one basket is extremely risky. With retirement at stake, most of us cannot afford a major mistake.

Useful websites

To find historical prices on the stock market: Go to Yahoo's finance website at <http://finance.yahoo.com/>.

To find historical prime lending rates: Go to <www.bankofcanada.ca/en/interest-look.htm>.

Timing Is Everything

Analyzing the rate of return in the stock market is a pretty tough thing to do. Because of its volatility, the timing of the measurement can lead to some pretty bizarre results.

Consider the euphoria leading up to the crash of 2000. The average yearly rate of return from July 1990 to July 2000 on the s&p/tsx was 11.32 percent. But the reason the 10-year average looks so good is because of one great year. During the year ending July 2000, the index increased 45.5 percent. The next year, it declined by 26 percent.

Doing the calculation over a period of many years gives the false impression that the returns are consistent. Absolutely nothing could be further from the truth. If you look at the returns of any stock market, you'll see a similar trait. They are all over the map from one year to the next. There seems to be no logic to them. This situation allows the investment companies to play a game with us.

When the markets are booming, rate of return information is all over the place. Ads for mutual funds tout detailed information: one-year, two-year, five-year, ten-year returns. Look how great our managers are! Why don't you see these ads during a bear market? Because it wouldn't be good for their business.

When is the right time to get into the market? Probably when the market is at a low point rather than a peak. However, most people tend to buy when everyone else is getting rich overnight. Who can resist when you hear that someone without investing experience made more than his or her annual salary in the market the previous month?

Assuming you want to get into the market, which month is best? October is one of the riskiest months to invest. The others are January to September, November, and December!

Will the Future Be Like the Past?

The common thinking is that the stock market will rebound because it always has. But the question is, how long will it take?

What if returns over the next 10 to 20 years don't reach the historical rates of the past? What will happen if there is a bear market for that period of time, and you generate only a 3 percent return per year on average, even with the risk? Anyone who puts all his or her eggs in the RRSP investment basket will be in for a very tough ride.

If you think that scenario is unlikely, just look at the situation in Japan. The Nikkei 225 index (look up symbol "^N225" at <finance.yahoo.com>) has declined from 20,449 in July 1994 to 11,187 in July 2004. That's a total decline of 45 percent, and a negative annual return of 5.9 percent. That couldn't happen in North America . . . or could it?

Alternatives to Mutual Funds

There is no easy answer to how to invest. Some of us will never feel comfortable making our own investment decisions. For others, education is the key to gaining the confidence to take control of their investments. Spend time researching alternatives such as exchange-traded index funds. These are investments like stocks and they are listed on the stock exchanges. They simply invest in the companies that the major indices do. They do have management expenses, but they are not mutual funds, and as a result, the expenses are much lower.

Don't like stocks at all? Spend time investigating the fixed income market — GICs, term deposits, bonds, etc. Here's something to get you started: the average five-year GIC interest rate from July 1994 to June 2004 was 4.85 percent. The highest rate during that period was 8.63 percent in January 1995. The lowest was 2.38 percent in March of 2004. In June of 2004, the average rate was up to 3.38 percent. With interest rates at historical lows recently, it's not surprising they seem to be heading up. If you could lock in an average rate of return between now and your retirement at rates averaging, say, 5 percent, with no risk and no fees, would you?

The answer to the question "What should I invest in?" will depend on many factors: your aversion to risk, your age, inflation data, etc. The best answer for most people is probably a mix of low-cost equities and fixed income investments. The only thing that's certain is that the more you educate yourself about the options, the better off you'll be.

YOUR PERSONAL RATE OF RETURN
What Those Investment Statements Don't Tell You

It has always bewildered me why most investment companies send monthly statements that focus on the short term. What is the point of showing what the market value of your investments was last month and what it is this month? The focus should be on the long term. After all, you are investing for your retirement, and what's longer than that?

What they should tell you, but don't, is the annual rate of return on your portfolio for periods including year-to-date, the last year, and since you opened the account. You should also be provided with benchmark rates of returns for different investment types, both domestically and internationally, so you can determine how you are doing in relative terms. Additionally, you should be informed of the cost of your investments so you can compare it to the current market value to see how many dollars you have gained or lost on each investment.

The problem is that the investment companies really don't want you to know this information, because your actual results may not be as rosy as those published numbers for the funds in which you may have some money invested. In most cases, you won't find any cost figures on your non-RRSP accounts, because they aren't forced to provide it.

Even if you have an unusual investment company that does provide some rate of return information, you may not be getting the whole story if you have more than one brokerage account. You need information on your investments as a whole, not just on one account. The big picture is what's important. For example, say you have two accounts with one broker, a discount brokerage account with someone else, and your spouse has one account at a third broker. Even if one or two of those investment companies provide rate of return information, you won't get the rate of return on all the investments put together. That's the only figure that's important to you: *your own personal rate of return.*

Who's going to calculate that figure? You are, and I'll show how to do it right now.

Your Rate of Return Calculator

I have written a simple Microsoft *Excel* program called the Personal Rate of Return (PRR) calculator (included on the CD-ROM with this book) that uses a function built into the program called Solver to provide the figures that really matter. All you need is the dollar amounts and dates you invested, and the current market value. It's as simple as that. You don't need to concern yourself with stock splits, dividend re-investments, or mutual fund disbursements to compute your effective annual rate of return.

Let's look at an example. Suppose you diligently started making RRSP contributions ten years ago. Some years you put in more, and sometimes, when cash was tight, you put in less. Some years you left your contribution until the last day, and other times you didn't. You have several different broker accounts, some in stocks and others in various mutual funds with different commission load structures.

You enter all the contribution amounts and dates in the spreadsheet. (The best way to get this information is to go through your old tax returns, since all the information is in one place rather than spread over many brokerage accounts.) You also know the total market value of all your RRSP accounts at December 31, 2004 — $100,000, in this example (see Figure 1) — but you will not enter that figure until you reach the "Solver" step of the program, which is explained in the box below.

The first thing to notice is that the market value of your investments is greater than the total cost of $94,200. Congratulations! You have a positive rate of return. (Don't laugh. In many cases, RRSP accounts are worth less than the actual dollars put into them.) But what rate of return have you received over the years?

Solver says . . . 1.12 percent per year. Do your own calculation and put yourself in a much better position to decide whether to pay off your debts or continue with the RRSP strategy.

How to Use the PRR Calculator

The program computes the effective annual rate, which takes into account the compounding period. All you need to know is the dollar amount and dates you originally invested, as well as the total current market value of all the related portfolios. The cells in which you need to input information are shown in bold typeface. All other cells are calculated by the program.

To use the program, you will need to have the Solver add-in to the Microsoft *Excel* program. Unfortunately, it usually doesn't come pre-installed. If you select "Tools" and see "Solver . . . " as a choice, you're ready to go. If not, here's how to install it:

- From the "Tools" menu, select "Add-Ins."
- In the "Add-Ins available" box, select "Solver Add-In."
- A box will come up saying, "Microsoft Excel can't run this add-in. This feature is not currently installed. Would you like to install it now?" Click "Yes."

- Excel may say that the feature you are trying to use is on a CD-ROM that is not available. Insert the CD that has *Excel* on it, and it will search for the needed file.
- Click "OK" and the solver should be installed.

Here's how it works following the example shown in Figure 1:

- Enter the date to which calculations are done in cell E6. That's the date that you have the current market value of all investments. Enter "31/12/2004" or "12/31/2004" depending on how your dates are displayed.
- Enter your original investment amounts in cells C12 to C24. If you need more lines, simply insert a line in *Excel* and copy the formulas from cells D and E in the line above.
- The program totals all your original contributions in cell C27. In this case it's $94,200.
- It will also calculate the final total market value in cell E29, which won't agree to your actual total until after the next step.

Now the solver comes in:

- Select "Tools" and then "Solver. . . . "
- In the "Set Target Cell:" box, enter E29 or simply click on that cell. (*Excel* will put a $ sign before the letter and the number. Don't worry about that.)
- After "Equal to:" select the "Value of:" button and enter the total current market value of "100,000" in this example.
- In the "By Changing Cells:" box, enter E33 or just click on that cell.
- Click on the "Solve" button, and there's your answer: 1.12 percent.

The program works backward to solve for the rate of return that would bring your original investments up to the current market value.

You have the option of keeping the Solver solution or restoring the original values in the program. Keep the Solver solution if you wish and just save the file under another name. This way, you will keep the original program intact so you can start from scratch later.

And if your broker says that it's too complicated for him or her to calculate the rate of return on your portfolio or that you wouldn't understand the complexities involved, bring your spreadsheet to the next meeting.

SUMMARY

You're back to that all-important decision: investing versus paying down debt. Here are the steps you should take:

1. Use the PRR Calculator to calculate your RRSP average rate of return since inception.

2. Consider whether returns in the future will be as good.

3. List all your personal debts, including the interest rates.

4. Compare your expected RRSP returns to the rates on your debt. If the rates on your debt exceed what you think you'll earn in your RRSP, start attacking debt instead of handing any more money to your adviser.

Without the figure from Step 1, you're open to the smoke and mirrors so expertly used by many in the investment community to secure their own financial futures at your expense. Don't let that happen. Use the tools at your disposal to make the right decision for you and your family.

Figure 1
CALCULATING YOUR PERSONAL RATE OF RETURN

	A	B	C	D	E
1					
2					
3					
4					
5					
6	ENTER DATE TO WHICH CALCULATIONS DONE IN CELL E6				12/31/04
7					
8		Date	Amount	# of days	Value
9		contributed	contributed	to calculation	at calculation
10				date	date
11					
12	Enter date and amount in columns B & C	2/28/92	0.00	4690	0.00
13	Cells in columns D & E are calculated	2/28/93	0.00	4324	0.00
14		1/22/94	6,500.00	3996	7,342.70
15		7/28/95	8,000.00	3444	8,886.26
16		12/02/96	3,700.00	2951	4,048.55
17		8/14/97	10,600.00	2696	11,508.66
18		4/30/98	7,500.00	2437	8,078.83
19		7/31/99	10,000.00	1980	10,622.65
20		1/28/00	10,500.00	1799	11,092.36
21		1/10/01	9,700.00	1451	10,139.02
22		2/25/02	8,700.00	1040	8,980.45
23		1/31/03	10,000.00	700	10,215.84
24		2/28/04	9,000.00	307	9,084.69
25					
26					
27	Total contributions		94,200.00		
28					
29	FINAL TOTAL MARKET VALUE (should agree to statement)				100,000.00
30					
31	GROWTH DOLLAR AMOUNT OVER CONTRIBUTIONS				5,800.00
32					
33	AVERAGE ANNUAL INTERNAL RATE OF RETURN (calculated)				1.12%

An Investment Primer

Before you put your money anywhere, be sure you understand the three basic principles of successful investing:

1. **Asset allocation**

   Asset allocation is one of the keys to effective investing, and it's a simple concept. All it means is don't put all your eggs in one basket. If you do, you are assuming a huge amount of risk. Think back to January 2000. If you had sold everything you owned and put the proceeds solely in dot-com start-up companies, where would you be now? Put politely, that would have been an ineffective asset-allocation strategy.

2. **Diversify by geography and investment type**

   With RRSPs, you should consider investing the maximum 30 percent outside Canada. Even if the Canadian market does well between now and your retirement, other countries may do even better.

   With equities, you are assuming more risk because there is no guarantee that you will be able to sell your investment later for more than you bought it for. In the worst case scenario, the company will go bankrupt, and you will get nothing. However, you might do well.

3. **Make changes as you age**

   The older you are, the less risk you should be willing to take, because after your earnings stream is cut off, you can't afford a major decline in your investment value. You need to ensure you have sufficient funds to live.

5

MYTH 4:
WE HAVE MET THE
ENEMY, AND HE IS
THE TAX COLLECTOR
(WITH APOLOGIES TO
WALTER KELLY)

EXPOSING THE MYTH

Don't get me wrong. I'm not saying that you should enjoy paying your taxes. In fact, it's your right to reduce your taxes by legitimate means wherever possible. What I am saying is you shouldn't make financial decisions for tax reasons; you should make them for economic reasons, giving consideration to the tax effect of the situation.

Too often, a strong dislike of taxes leads unwary consumers into investing in misguided tax shelters, making poor decisions about when to sell in the stock market, and making the ill-conceived decision to borrow to invest. Let's look at the reality.

Tax Shelters Я Us

Tax shelters are number one on the list of products that prey on consumers' dislike for paying taxes. High-income earners, such as professional athletes, doctors, and lawyers,

73

fall for this ploy time and time again. Investing in tax shelters is like playing the lottery. You may strike it rich, but odds are you'll lose — perhaps big time.

Here's the usual pitch: "Invest $10,000 in XYZ partnership and you'll get a $10,000 tax deduction! You could save more than $4,600 in taxes this year!"

That's great — if you get the $10,000 back later. The problem is that in the majority of cases, you won't. You may not get anything back. And if you don't, you have just thrown away $5,400 (in this example) or more, depending on your tax bracket. That's why the government is giving you the big tax break — because of the risk you are taking.

Why does the government allow these tax shelter schemes to exist? Mainly to encourage investment in certain industries. But you have to be aware also that the government does *not* support every tax shelter out there. The government looks very closely at tax shelters because many are simply shams. It has been known to go back years and disallow deductions because a tax shelter turned out to be something less than legitimate.

If in the above example your deduction was disallowed, you would have lost the whole thing — not just $5,400, but $10,000 of your hard-earned cash. And if you had borrowed to make the investment, you would be making those loan payments for years to come and getting nothing in return.

Even worse, when the government reassesses your tax return, they will add interest to the additional taxes owing. In other words, you'll owe them the $4,600 in taxes, plus interest at the "prescribed interest rate" for every day since the taxes were originally due. (The prescribed interest rate is set quarterly by the government, and it is usually higher than the bank's prime rate.) Oh, and by the way, this interest isn't tax deductible.

It's not just traditional tax shelters that you have to watch out for. Let me give you an example.

Beware: Tax Shelter Ahead!

Near the end of December a couple of years ago, I started seeing ads in the paper for an "investment opportunity," but I had to hurry as there were only "four days left." On December 29, I decided to see what was being offered.

A well-known investment speaker was making a presentation about an "opportunity" to invest in a donation scheme. The reason for the big rush was because donations are deductible only if made by the end of the calendar year. During the presentation, videos and articles by esteemed professionals, including lawyers and accountants, were put forth that claimed the government was on board with the scheme and that the group would fight any attempt to disallow the tax credits offered. They even had a $425,000 "defence fund" to fight the government if it changed its mind.

This is how it worked: If you invested $10,000, they would give you a donation receipt for $56,522 "based on fair market value." The money was being invested in comic books that would be used to help kids in developing countries learn to read. The group would buy the comic books in bulk and get a discount on the price, so that your $10,000 would actually buy $56,522 worth of comic books. Their calculations showed that you would receive a net tax credit of $15,427 — more than your original investment.

If you fell for this "opportunity," you may be one of the unlucky 5,000 Canadians who have already had their donations disallowed, or you may be one of the next 5,000 currently being audited. I hope not, because in many cases, the government is not only eliminating the donation, it is also assessing a 50 percent penalty for gross negligence.

Don't Sell: The Taxes Will Kill You

It has been said investment decisions are based on two emotions: fear and greed. When the stock market is declining, fear drives people to sell and stop their losses. When the market is climbing, they hold onto their stocks hoping they'll go higher. Taxes can play a role in compounding the problem. A simple example from recent history will explain this.

Say you owned $1 million worth of Nortel stock at the peak of the market. That would have been 8,400 shares at about $120, equalling $1,008,000. At the time, you thought it might still go higher, so you waited. However, you called your accountant to see what the taxes would be just in case you did decide to sell. You had bought the stock at $25 per share, so your cost base was $210,000 (8,400 shares x $25). Your capital gain would have been the difference between the proceeds and the cost base: in this case, $798,000.

Capital gains get favorable tax treatment — only 50 percent of the actual gain is taxed — so $399,000 would be added to your personal income tax return. Even if your salary was low, the amount would put the majority of the taxable capital gain in the top bracket. At a 46 percent marginal tax rate, you would have owed about $183,540 in taxes. "Get out!," you screamed at your accountant at the time, and you sat tight.

Today, with the stock around $5, your portfolio is worth $42,000, and you no longer have a tax problem. Maybe you should have been less worried about those taxes!

Borrow Your Way to Riches — Or Rags

Some financial advisers promote the idea of borrowing to invest because the interest is tax deductible (for investments outside an RRSP). Once again, they are playing on your dislike of taxes, but they're not revealing the risk associated with such a strategy.

Don't fall for this ploy. With a debt pay-down strategy, adding to your personal debt is a sin. If you have to borrow for a vacation, you are sacrificing your future for the present. You may think that borrowing to invest isn't that bad, because you are using "leverage" to increase your net worth. Right? Well, you may find an investment that does well. Alternatively, you could end up broke.

Recent rates at a Canadian chartered bank tell the tale of how things are stacked against you. A five-year fixed term deposit pays 2.8 percent per year, while a five-year mortgage at the same institution costs 5.8 percent annually. That difference of 3 percent is called the "spread," and it's the way banks make much of their money. Since you're not the bank, you're working against the spread, and that's an uphill battle.

Can you imagine what the people who borrowed to invest in Nortel at the peak are wishing now? They will essentially have a mortgage on their future with no house attached. The concept is simple: debt allows you to get into big trouble because you are risking more than you have. Unless you want to play the lottery with your family's future, don't do it.

THE ALTERNATIVE: FOCUS ON NET WORTH, NOT TAXES

The problem with focusing on minimizing taxes is clear: it clouds your judgment and takes your attention away from other areas of your personal finances that could benefit you far more than saving a few tax dollars.

If you focus on building your net worth instead of just minimizing taxes, you'll likely make much wiser financial decisions. Spend more time thinking about in which location you should buy your next house. Is it a good area? Do prices rise at a greater rate than one of your other options? When it comes time to sell, you'll have more cash in your pocket to put down on your next house.

If you own a business, focus on increasing its value. Your business has the potential to be a substantial portion of your total net worth and is a great way for you to provide funds for yourself after your retirement. You may be able to sell it or continue to take a salary or dividends after you stop working.

Once you start thinking this way, you'll probably come up with some of your own personal ideas — ideas that could make or save you a lot of money.

SUMMARY

Focusing on your net worth is the key to making sound decisions, especially when it comes to taxes. If you do that, you will probably come to the same conclusions I have. Let's summarize:

- Investing in a tax shelter, no matter what your income level, is rarely a sound financial strategy.

- Don't borrow to invest in or outside an RRSP.

- Never avoid the sale of an asset that has appreciated because you fear the tax bill.

6

MYTH 5:
SECURE YOUR
FINANCIAL FUTURE:
BUY LIFE INSURANCE

EXPOSING THE MYTH

For years, we've been exposed to ads from a certain insurance company about retiring early. The message is that if you buy insurance from them, they will make your dreams come true. If you put your trust in them, retirement at 55 is possible.

Now think about this: What has life insurance got to do with financial freedom? You won't achieve financial freedom. You'll be dead!

Life insurance has its purpose: It should allow a family to maintain their standard of living if the breadwinner were to die. If you talk to many life insurance agents however, you may get a different idea. The myths they perpetuate could cost you dearly.

The truth is that if you don't have any dependants, you really don't need any life insurance at all. If you have young children, you probably do need it. It boils down to what life would be like for your family without you.

Say you are a 35-year-old sole income-earner, with a spouse and two young children. If you were to die, what would they do? You probably wouldn't have a lot of money saved to sustain them for the rest of their lives. How would they pay for food, clothing, and shelter? You'd better have life insurance.

If, however, you have a working spouse but no children, why do you need life insurance? If you die, your spouse would probably continue working. Does it make sense for you to pay life insurance premiums so that if you die, your spouse's new companion can live off the death benefit and won't ever have to work?

Some agents will even try to convince you to insure the lives of your children. If your agent tries this, get another agent. The death of a child is probably the worst thing that could happen to a person. Is a lump sum of money really going to help? I don't think so.

THE CASE AGAINST WHOLE LIFE AND UNIVERSAL LIFE INSURANCE

The box on pages 88 and 89 defines the three basic types of insurance available today: term, universal, and whole life. If you aren't familiar with these terms, take the time to review them now.

Many agents will try to sell you a universal life or a whole life insurance policy because of the "savings" component. They claim that you'll be building up savings at the same time as you cover your life. Don't fall for this argument! Let's look at the reasons why.

You Can't Have It Both Ways

With both whole and universal life insurance, you must remember this: You don't get the cash surrender value *and* the death benefit; you get the cash surrender value *or* the death benefit. The death benefit applies if the insured dies, and the cash surrender value applies if you cancel the policy.

In other words, the cash surrender value is being used to fund the death benefit. That's extremely important to keep in mind when you are looking at those fancy projections designed to sell you on these types of policies.

If You Cancel It, It's Not Tax-Free

If you cancel a whole or universal life insurance policy, you'll be taxed on the difference between the cash surrender value received and the cost base of the policy (the total premiums paid, less dividends received).

How Do Your Savings Grow?

Let's take a look at how effective the rate of return is on the savings invested in a life insurance policy. This is best explained by Kwok Ho and Chris Robinson in their excellent book, *Personal Financial Planning* (Captus Press, 2001):

> *Empirical studies in the past find that the rate of return on whole life is inferior to that available on comparable savings instruments. In other words, there is evidence that you would earn a higher return by putting the monetary "difference" in a chartered bank savings account than by putting it in whole life insurance. But why is that the case? We think this is due, to a large extent, to the high commission fees that insurance companies pay to agents. In general, the insurance companies pay a much higher commission fee to agents for selling whole life than they do for selling individual term*

life. Since the commission is a percentage on the total premium that you pay, this means that you pay a commission for saving money with an insurance company. Banks do not charge you a commission for putting your money into a savings account!" *

How Big Is That Commission, Anyway?

If you have a whole life policy, you've paid thousands of dollars in premiums in a year, much more than what you would have paid for term insurance. Just look at the cash surrender value at the end of the first year. In many cases, it's close to zero. That's because the insurance agent's commission is often equal to almost all of the premiums you pay in that first year. Now you know why they are so aggressive.

When Will the Premiums Stop?

There are other significant risks with a whole life policy. First of all, the premiums are not guaranteed. They could be extended for many years beyond what the charts show or even increased if the insurance company does not do as well as expected on its investments. Read the fine print and you'll see words like the following: "There is NO guarantee that regular premium payments and dump-ins can cease after eight years."

There is also no guarantee that the investment component will do better than the "guaranteed minimum" return. Insurance agents often state this by saying something like, "The primary example is based on the current dividend scale, which is not guaranteed."

Whole life policies are not at all flexible. The full premiums are due no matter what. At least with a universal life

*Excerpted from *Personal Financial Planning*. 3rd ed., by Kwok Ho and Chris Robinson (Concord, Ontario: Captus Press Inc., 2001). Reprinted with permission of Captus Press Inc., Units 14 & 15, 1600 Steeles Ave. West, Concord, ON L4K 4M2. E-mail: <Info@captus.com>, Internet: <http://www.captus.com>.

policy you can pay the pure cost of insurance out of dividends generated in the policy.

In short, it's difficult to make a strong independent recommendation for whole life insurance.

HOW MUCH COVERAGE DO YOU NEED?

Now that we've exploded the myths of life insurance, let's look at how to determine the amount of coverage you should have.

Many people decide how much insurance to get because they are sold a policy by an aggressive salesperson. Here's one pitch I have heard:

- *Step 1:* Add up all your personal debt, including credit cards, lines of credit, mortgage, and car loans.

- *Step 2:* Determine the amount of money you would need to invest to replace the annual salary of the insured person.

- *Step 3:* Add the two amounts together, and that's the amount of coverage you need.

Let's throw some numbers in and see what happens using this method.

A couple, Bob and Sarah Simpson, have one child, Jeff, age five, and personal debt totalling $250,000, including a mortgage. Bob is the only breadwinner, and he makes $90,000 per year. Assuming an average rate of return of 5 percent, $1.8 million would be needed to generate $90,000 per year. Bob would need to insure himself for $2.05 million ($250,000 + $1.8 million), according to the pitch. If Bob qualifies, that's quite a hefty amount of coverage and would be very costly.

Are the Simpsons being well advised or is the sales person just doing a great selling job? Let's see.

First of all, they do need life insurance on Bob because if he were to die, Sarah and Jeff would otherwise be in dire straights. But how much do they need?

There are two ways to determine the amount of coverage required: the income-replacement method and the expense-projection method. The former focuses on replacing the income that will be lost, and the latter focuses on the future expenses that need to be covered. Unfortunately, like most Canadian families, the Simpsons don't keep detailed records of their spending. They are therefore forced to focus on income replacement rather than the more accurate expense-projection method.

The Income-Replacement Method

With the income-replacement method, in our example, if Sarah were to receive $1.8 million on Bob's death, it would pay her $90,000 per year at 5 percent. As we saw in Chapter 2, this is a neat trick that is often used, but it's deceiving in its simplicity. Sarah would get the $90,000 every year and she would also be left with the $1.8 million intact when she died.

Assume Sarah is 35 years old when Bob dies. To provide $90,000 per year, assuming a 5 percent rate of return on the investments for the next 30 years, she could buy an annuity for $1.4 million. That amount would yield $90,000 for 30 years. This is the time period that Bob would have been working had he lived.

But there is another important point to consider: taxes. The face value of a policy is received tax-free, since life insurance premiums are not tax deductible, and that makes a big difference. Bob would have been reporting the $90,000 per year as salary income and would have been paying income tax on the full amount if he had lived. Sarah would not have to include the $1.4 million death benefit in her income. She would, however, pay taxes on any interest earned on the face amount after it is paid out, but that would be much less than what Bob would have paid.

Look at it this way: Sarah would receive $2.7 million over the next 30 years ($90,000 x 30), but $1.4 million of that would simply be a return of her capital and therefore not taxed. Over the 30 years she would be paying tax on the difference ($1.3 million), whereas Bob would have paid tax on the whole $2.7 million. That means she would need a lot less coverage than the $1.4 million to be in the same position as Bob on an after-tax basis.

Many in the insurance industry use a factor of 75 percent to compensate for this tax issue. That is, they recommend you insure to replace only 75 percent of the lost income. In this case, 75 percent of $90,000 is $67,500. Sarah would still need $1.04 million of coverage to provide that much per year for 30 years at 5 percent. That's about half the amount the sales representative was pushing, but it is still a formidable amount.

The Expense-Projection Method

If the Simpsons diligently tracked their expenses, they could use the expense-projection method. With detailed information about past and current spending, it's not that difficult to project future spending. They would then probably notice several important things.

First of all, without Bob, their expenses would decline. There would be one less mouth to feed every day. They would need only one car. Sarah and Jeff wouldn't require as much space and would have the option of downsizing the house. They would need to save less for retirement. Jeff will soon be six years old and starting grade 1. That will leave Sarah more time perhaps to get a job. She may even find another mate who already earns an income.

All these factors should be taken into consideration. The conclusion could very well be that a much lower amount of insurance is required.

Now assume that Sarah is already keen to get back to work. If they insured Bob for $250,000, the total amount of their debt, she would be able to clear it all if he died. As we saw in Chapter 2, if you have no debt, your expenses decline significantly. Even if Sarah doesn't earn as much as Bob does, she may be able to maintain her standard of living quite well upon his death.

SUMMARY

Everyone's personal financial situation is different. There are no "right answers." If you don't have a good idea of where your money is going, you are leaving yourself vulnerable to the "rule of thumb" selling methods used by some less-than-objective agents. You can do better than that.

Understanding Insurance Basics

Beneficiary: The person to whom a death benefit is paid after the death of an insured person.

Face value: The amount received by the beneficiary upon the death of the insured. Also known as the *death benefit*.

Insurability: Whether or not a person qualifies for insurance. In most cases, a medical exam is required to determine whether or not an insurance company will assume the risk of insuring someone.

Owner: The person who pays the insurance premiums. This can be the insured, another person, or even a company.

Premium: The amount paid to the insurance company, usually on a monthly or annual basis.

Policy term: The period covered by the insurance policy. This can range from one year to a lifetime.

Rate: The cost of each unit of insurance. For example, a rate of $1.50 per $100 unit would translate to $375 annual cost for a $25,000 face value policy ($25,000/$100 x $1.50).

Types of insurance available:

1. **Term life:** A pure life insurance policy without any savings/investment features.

2. **Universal life:** A combination of term life insurance and a separate investment fund. As long as you pay the insurance portion of the premium each year, the policy remains in force. These policies are flexible because the amount accumulated in the investment fund can be used to pay the premium required to maintain the policy if you can't afford to do so.

3. **Whole life:** Similar to universal life, except the premiums are not segregated into an insurance premium and a savings component. You are leaving it up to the insurance company to handle all aspects of the policy, including the investments.

A term policy will have a much lower premium that increases with age. As you get older, the premiums become very expensive, to the point at which it does not make sense to continue coverage.

Policies with an investment component have premiums for a fixed period of time that eventually stop, even though the insurance coverage continues. You pay more than the required amount for the insurance coverage in the beginning, and less than the required amount toward the end of the policy. The excess funds in the early years are invested and accumulated by the insurance company. This is what's called the "cash surrender value" (csv). If you cancel the policy, the cash surrender value is what will be returned to you. These types of policies are just a combination of term insurance and an investment account where the investment portion is used up in future years to pay for the coverage. They will pay the death benefit, assuming you continue to pay all the required premiums.

PART TWO

FIGHTING BACK

7

THE RRSP TRAP: OPTIMIZE, DON'T MAXIMIZE

The RRSP Trap

Like many of us in the post-dot-com era, you've conceded that you probably aren't going to retire a multi-millionaire. You just want to have a reasonable amount put away to ensure your golden years are comfortable. How much of an RRSP are you going to need? $300,000? $650,000? $1 million? If you're like many Canadians, you simply have no idea. Unfortunately, the answer is not as easy as applying a rule of thumb, because we each have a financial situation that is as individual as our fingerprints.

How Much Money Will You Need?

Imagine for a minute that you are a track and field athlete entering the Olympic Games. Your specialty is running. You show up at the stadium for your race, but there's a problem: you have no idea how long the race is. Are you entered in the 100-yard dash or a marathon? It obviously makes a huge difference to how you should have trained for the event. Training for a marathon isn't going to help much in a race that's over in 9.79 seconds.

That's how many people approach retirement. They know they are going to be in an event when they retire. In this case, the event is money planning, and most people aren't that good at it. To take a page from one of my favourite books, *The Seven Habits of Highly Effective People* (Stephen R. Covey, Simon & Schuster), the best way to play this game is to begin with the end in mind. That is, determine about how much money you will spend each year, how long you are likely to live, and work backwards to determine how big your RRSP needs to be.

Without this personal information, what do most people do? They assume the maximum RRSP contribution levels are what they'll need to invest each year to secure their retirement. This could be a major mistake. Let's dig deeper to find out why.

RRSP Problem 1: Age 69

The mandatory age at which you must convert your RRSP into retirement income was 71 for 1996 and prior years. Since 1997, however, that age was reduced to 69. Why? Because the government wants you to pay taxes earlier.

The new rules state that during the year you turn 69, you must convert your RRSP to a Registered Retirement Income Fund (RRIF) or annuity and begin withdrawing set amounts by December 31 of the next year. That next year, you will still be 69 at the beginning of the year and will turn 70 during the year. (Note that the RRIF rules are based on your age at the beginning of the year, not the age you turn during the year.) The minimum RRIF withdrawal percentage for the year you are 69 at the beginning is 4.76 percent of the opening market value of the RRIF. The next year, it's

5 percent. These percentages are based on the formula 1/(90-age) so 1/(90-69) = 0.0476 for the year you start at age 69 and 1/(90-70) = 0.05 for the year you start at age 70.

Be careful not to miss those first two years, as many of the minimum RRIF charts start at age 71. Also remember that if you have a younger spouse you can, if you can afford to, base the minimum withdrawal percentages on his or her age for the mandatory withdrawals.

For the years when you are 71 to 77 at the beginning, the formula no longer works for RRIFs opened after 1992. The rates have been set by the government and, as you probably guessed, they are higher than they otherwise would be. For example, for the year during which you are 71 at the beginning (and turn 72 during), the rate is 7.38 percent not 5.26 percent, as the formula would dictate. Again, it's a way of getting more tax revenue out of your pockets sooner. The fixed percentage rises to 8.15 percent in the year you start at age 77 (the formula would dictate 7.69 percent in that year). For the year you start at age 78 and older, the rates are set by the government and gradually increase to 20 percent at age 94 and above.

One of the problems with these rules is that they penalize people who have their finances under control. What if you don't need that much money to live the way you would like? You don't have a choice; you must withdraw the minimum amount and pay tax on it.

Let's consider an example.

If you had a RRIF worth $1,000,000 at the beginning of the year you started at age 71, you would have to withdraw $73,800. What if you could get along comfortably on $50,000 because you have no debt, you own your cars and your kids are self-sufficient? You would have to pay tax on the extra $23,800 anyway, and that's about $8,100 at current 2004 Ontario rates.

The second problem is that a large RRIF may lead to clawbacks of the Old Age Security (OAS) pension.

In the above example, even without any other income (CPP, investments, etc.) the feds would have clawed back $2,101.50 (15 percent of the excess above $59,790 in 2004). I don't know about you, but giving away free money doesn't sound like a good strategy to me.

RRSP Problem 2: Death

As long as you name your spouse or common-law partner as the successor annuitant in the terms of your RRIF contract or your will, your RRIF payments will continue to be paid to him or her after your death. Upon the demise of your spouse, however, the entire remaining balance of your RRIF comes into income on his or her final tax return, along with the balance of his or her RRIF. (There is an exception for financially dependent children or grandchildren.) Often, the majority of this is at a high rate of tax.

For example, say the RRIFs had a fair market value of $400,000 immediately before the death of your surviving spouse. Even if he or she had no other income, the tax bill in Ontario would be about $168,000 in 2004.

Let's look at a scenario to see the effect of the OAS clawback and the taxation of RRIFs upon death.

Meet Jim Bradley

Jim Bradley was born on January 2, 1960, and is therefore 44 years old in 2004. Jim is good at what he does to earn income, but by his own admission, he lacks financial expertise. Securing his retirement years is simple in his mind, since it's what he's been hearing since he was a kid: maximize RRSP contributions each and every year, no matter what. He has been doing just that since he was 30 years old.

(Okay, so if he had been really listening, he would have started at age 22; but he resisted and enjoyed the next eight years free of worry about retirement.)

In 1990, when he turned 30, he contributed the maximum RRSP allowed — $7,500. He continued doing that every year until 2004, where he contributed the maximum — $15,500 (allowed since he earned $100,000 in 2003). At an average annual rate of return of 5 percent, his RRSP portfolio will be worth $276,754 at December 31, 2004.

Assuming he puts in the allowed $16,500 in 2005, and $18,000 from 2006 until 2025 (when he turns 65), and that the portfolio grows at 5 percent a year on average, his RRSP will grow to a value of $1,409,995 at December 31, 2025.

He plans to retire when he is 65 and begin collecting the CPP and OAS pensions at that time.

Jim wishes to know the following:

- How much OAS pension will be clawed back after he retires?

- Will his minimum RRIF payments exceed what he'll need to live comfortably?

- What will his RRIF be worth upon his death?

- How much tax will be payable on the RRIF on his final tax return?

To answer Jim's questions, we need to make some assumptions. Let's do that now.

The Assumptions

- Jim is eligible for the maximum OAS pension, which at present is $5,600, and the amount will grow at the assumed inflation rate.

- Jim is eligible for the maximum CPP pension, which at present is $9,770, and the amount will grow at the assumed inflation rate.

- Jim will require approximately 50 percent of his last year's pre-retirement income to maintain his lifestyle after he retires because his mortgage will be paid off, his kids will have moved out, and he will no longer be saving for retirement. In today's dollars, that is $50,000 (2003 income of $100,000 x 50 percent). This amount is adjusted for inflation.

- Jim will not have any other income after retirement (i.e., from company pensions, self-employment income or investments outside his RRSP).

- The taxable income at which the OAS clawback begins is $59,790 in 2004, and this amount will increase at the assumed rate of inflation.

- Jim's RRSP/RRIF will earn an average of 4 percent per year after he retires, since he is shifting to more conservative investments.

- Inflation will average 2 percent per year from now until Jim dies.

- Jim will live until he is 82.

- His wife is the same age as Jim, and she does not outlive him.

- Federal and Ontario personal income taxes are calculated at 2003 rates.

The Results

Now let's look at Jim's spreadsheet, which is shown below as Figure 2.

Interestingly enough, the clawback of the OAS pension does not seem to be much of a problem for Jim except for the years when he is between the ages of 72 and 79, starting at $4,331 and declining to practically zero during that period. Interestingly, that coincides with the increased RRIF percentages under the new rules.

The real problems arise when we look at some of the other columns. Have a look at the amount of RRIF income Jim will have to withdraw above what he has determined he'll need in the year he turns 72. The Total Income after Additional RRIF is $132,970. This amount includes the minimum RRIF payment, OAS and CPP pensions (there is no additional RRIF income required in this case). Now look at the Required Income — $87,051. (For the technically inclined, that's 50 percent of the future value of his current salary of $100,000 for 28 years at 2 percent inflation per year). The difference is $45,919. That's extra income that Jim will have to withdraw and pay tax on, even though he doesn't need the money. Look at the Excess Income column on the far right. It shows the real problem with RRSPs that are too large. In Jim's case, from age 70 to 82, he will be forced to withdraw and pay tax on more than $331,000 of money he doesn't even need.

What about when Jim dies? If he dies at age 82, his RRIF will still be worth $878,732, and that'll cost him about $408,000 in taxes. Currently Canadian males live on average for 75.2 years, while females live for 81.2 years. What if he dies at 75? His RRIF will be worth an astounding $1,231,362. The tax bill on that? About $571,000.

Your personal situation will almost certainly be different than Jim's, but there is a useful lesson that can be learned: perhaps you should concentrate on optimizing the amount of your RRSP rather than trying to maximize it.

How to Avoid the RRSP Trap

Let's take a look at what Jim Bradley could do to avoid the RRSP trap. Let's start by looking at the positive things that

Figure 2
RETIREMENT OPTIMIZER

RRSP YEARS

Age During Year**	RRSP Value Beginning of Year	RRSP Withdrawals	Increase in RRSP Value During Year	RRSP Value End of Year	OAS Payments*	CPP Payments*
55	$0	$0	$0	$0		
56	$0	$0	$0	$0		
57	$0	$0	$0	$0		
58	$0	$0	$0	$0		
59	$0	$0	$0	$0		
60	$0	$0	$0	$0		
61	$0	$0	$0	$0		
62	$0	$0	$0	$0		
63	$0	$0	$0	$0		
64	$0	$0	$0	$0		
65	$1,409,995	$0	$56,400	$1,466,395	$7,719	$13,571
66	$1,466,395	$53,608	$56,511	$1,469,298	$8,589	$15,101
67	$1,469,298	$54,681	$56,585	$1,471,202	$8,761	$15,403
68	$1,471,202	$55,774	$56,617	$1,472,045	$8,936	$15,711
69	$1,472,045	$56,890	$56,606	$1,471,761	$9,115	$16,025

Other Income*	Total Income	OAS Clawback*	Total Income	Required Income*	RRSP on Death
$0	$0		$0	$0	$0
$0	$0		$0	$0	$0
$0	$0		$0	$0	$0
$0	$0		$0	$0	$0
$0	$0		$0	$0	$0
$0	$0		$0	$0	$0
$0	$0		$0	$0	$0
$0	$0		$0	$0	$0
$0	$0		$0	$0	$0
$0	$0		$0	$0	$0
$0	$21,291	$0	$21,291	$0	$0
$0	$77,299	$0	$77,299	$77,299	$0
$0	$78,845	$0	$78,845	$78,845	$0
$0	$80,422	$0	$80,422	$80,422	$0
$0	$82,030	$0	$82,030	$82,030	$0

Figure 2 — Continued

RRIF YEARS

Age During Year**	RRIF Value Beginning of Year	Minimum RRIF Withdrawals	Additional RRIF Withdrawal to meet Required Income	Increase in RRIF Value During Year	RRIF Value End of Year	OAS Payments*
70	1,471,761	70,084	0	56,067	1,457,745	9,298
71	1,457,745	72,887	0	55,394	1,440,252	9,483
72	1,440,252	106,291	0	53,358	1,387,320	9,673
73	1,387,320	103,772	0	51,342	1,334,890	9,867
74	1,334,890	101,318	0	49,343	1,282,915	10,064
75	1,282,915	98,913	0	47,360	1,231,362	10,265
76	1,231,362	96,662	0	45,388	1,180,088	10,471
77	1,180,088	94,289	0	43,432	1,129,231	10,680
78	1,129,231	92,032	0	41,488	1,078,687	10,894
79	1,078,687	89,855	0	39,553	1,028,385	11,111
80	1,028,385	87,721	0	37,627	978,291	11,334
81	978,291	85,600	0	35,708	928,398	11,560
82	928,398	83,463	0	33,797	878,732	11,791

* Amounts adjusted for inflation

** You must convert your RRSP to a RRIF in the year you turn 69. The next year you must make your first RRIF withdrawal before December 31. During this next year you are 69 at the beginning of the year and you turn 70 during the year.

CPP Payments*	Other Income*	Total Income Before Add. RRIF	Total Income After Add. RRIF	OAS Clawback*	Total Income	Required Income*	Excess Income
16,346	0	95,727	95,727	0	95,727	83,671	12,056
16,673	0	99,044	99,044	0	99,044	85,344	13,699
17,006	0	132,970	132,970	4,331	128,639	87,051	45,919
17,346	0	130,985	130,985	3,721	127,264	88,792	42,192
17,693	0	129,075	129,075	3,116	125,959	90,568	38,507
18,047	0	127,225	127,225	2,514	124,712	92,379	34,846
18,408	0	125,541	125,541	1,930	123,611	94,227	31,314
18,776	0	123,745	123,745	1,322	122,423	96,112	27,634
19,152	0	122,078	122,078	727	121,350	98,034	24,044
19,535	0	120,501	120,501	139	120,362	99,994	20,506
19,926	0	118,981	118,981	0	118,981	101,994	16,986
20,324	0	117,485	117,485	0	117,485	104,034	13,451
20,731	0	115,985	115,985	0	115,985	106,115	9,870
							331,024

Jim has going for him with his current strategy of maximizing his RRSP contributions. First of all, he is getting a tax refund on his RRSP contribution. In 2005, he can contribute the maximum $16,500 resulting in a tax refund of approximately $7,200, since his salary in 2005 will be $102,000 (a marginal tax rate of about 43 percent in Ontario).

Since he has already maximized his RRSP contributions, he can't reinvest these savings in an RRSP as we assumed the Harts did earlier. Good news for Jim — he gets to spend it on whatever he likes. For Jim, that's a European vacation each and every year. Obviously, there is some value in this situation. He is saving more than enough for retirement and getting a great vacation to boot, right? Well, yes. But is there perhaps a better way to do it?

We've seen the negatives of the situation — an RRSP that's so big at the end that Jim ends up having to withdraw more than he needs from his RRIF starting at age 70, clawbacks of the OAS pension, and resulting huge tax bill when he (or his spouse if she lives longer) dies. As we have also discussed, he is hoping for a 5 percent return on his RRSP investments, and may get that, but there are no guarantees.

Let's look at what Jim could do differently. If he reduces his RRSP contributions to $8,000 per year, his RRSP refund at 43 percent would be about $3,500. So instead of handing over $16,500 to his mutual fund salesperson and getting $7,200 back from the government (a net cash outflow of $9,300), he hands $8,000 over and gets $3,500 back, for a net outflow of $4,500.

Assuming he started with $16,500 available, the reduced RRSP option would leave him with $12,000. That's the extra $8,500 that he didn't hand over, plus the $3,500 tax refund. He has $4,800 more in hand than the maximum RRSP option. He can do whatever he likes with it. He could invest it in something other than an RRSP or choose to purchase something like a vacation property.

I can hear the mutual fund salespeople screaming already. But he's got an extra $8,500 working in his RRSP for him! What about the value of compound earnings? And what about the fact that the money is growing tax sheltered?

The result of all those "positives" is that he ends up with a huge RRSP that penalizes him because he has his finances under control and doesn't need all that money after retirement. Furthermore, he doesn't feel inclined to hand over half of what's left in his RRIF after he dies to the taxperson.

But let's not stop there. We need to know if Jim has enough to retire on with the reduced RRSP contributions. I have punched in Jim's new answers to the spreadsheet, and guess what? He's fine. His RRSP will still grow to $1,056,780, he will always meet his required income levels, and when he dies at age 82 his RRIF will still be worth $557,261.

The Retirement Optimizer Key Variables

There are some variables relating to retirement over which you have little control: inflation, the age you will pass to the great beyond, and income tax rates, to name a few. There are others, however, over which you have a great deal of control, such as the percentage of your current income that you will need after you retire.

As we have seen, if you retire debt-free with self-sufficient children and are in reasonably good physical shape, that percentage could be 50 percent or even lower. On the other hand, if you retire in debt up to your ears, lease cars, and have live-at-home kids, you could need even more than you make now! The choice is not easy, but it's yours to make.

There is also another variable that you control. It's whether you can, or will need to, earn income after you retire. Unfortunately for some, it will be a requirement. They simply won't have enough money put aside to survive. For others, it's worth giving some thought to.

What Are You Doing after Work?

No, I don't mean at 5:00 p.m. (or 7:00 p.m. or 8:00 p.m. if you are a workaholic); I mean after you stop working for good. I mean what are your hobbies? You'll need to do something to keep yourself busy, and that something you definitely have control over. It can also have a huge impact on how much money you'll need.

Think about your hobby: is it a cash generator, a cash drainer, or cash neutral? Many hobbies are cash drainers, including such things as travelling the world, becoming a wine connoisseur, or perhaps collecting fine art. There is absolutely nothing wrong with those hobbies; they'll just cost you more. Cash neutral (more or less) hobbies could include gardening (which is torture for me!), woodworking, automobile restoration, volunteering on non-profit boards, etc.

Cash-generating hobbies could include consulting in your area of expertise, lecturing, or perhaps writing or handyman activities. Sitting around the house all day would drive me nuts. I love dealing with money issues and hope to continue writing about it and helping clients and friends handle their money even after I stop working. That will be a source of funds for me. What about you?

Let's go back to Jim Bradley and plug in some numbers to see what happens. We'll assume that Jim feels he'll be able to earn $5,000 per year (in today's dollars) from age 66 to 69. That will reduce the amount he will need to withdraw from his RRSP during those years before he has to convert his RRSP to a RRIF. Let's say that because of this, he figures he can afford to reduce his RRSP contributions from $8,000 to $5,000 per year. The results?

His RRSP will be worth $949,623 at age 65, he will always meet his required income estimate, and his RRIF will still be worth $440,826 at age 82.

How to Optimize Your Own RRSP

Jim Bradley's case showed us that if we get our finances under control, we may not need to maximize our RRSP contributions. In Chapter 2, we looked at the Harts and showed how in some cases, it may be possible to finance our retirement years with a very small RRSP. Your case probably won't be like Jim Bradley or the Harts since you and your family are unique and your situation will change, sooner or later.

To help you, I have written a simple tool that is available to you right now. It's on the CD-ROM at the back of this book and it's easy to use. Install the program and click on the file Retirement Optimizer. (You will need to have *Microsoft Excel* installed on your computer.) After you open the file, all you have to do is answer the same questions that Jim Bradley did earlier in this chapter. The program will do the rest. Oh, and don't worry about accidentally deleting the wrong thing — the workbook is protected to prevent this.

Here's a list of the questions you'll need to answer:

- What is today's date?
- What is your first and last name?
- On what day were you born?
- What is the total market value of your RRSPs on the most recent statement?
- How much do you plan to contribute to your RRSP each year from now until retirement?

- At what age do you plan to retire and stop making RRSP contributions?

- At what annual rate of return do you expect your RRSP investments to grow until you retire?

- At what annual rate of return do you expect your RRSP or RRIF investments to grow after you retire?

- What average annual rate of inflation do you expect over the remainder of your life?

- Are you eligible for the maximum Old Age Security (OAS) pension at age 65?

- Are you eligible for the maximum Canada Pension Plan (CPP) pension at age 65?

- How much money from other sources in today's dollars do you expect each year after you retire? (For example, pension, self-employment, rental, and investments outside RRSPs.)

- At what age do you expect this income from other sources to stop?

- What is your current total income before taxes? (I.e., salary or net income from self-employment)

- What percentage of your income before tax in today's dollars do you think you will need after you retire?

- To what age do you think you will live? (**Note:** If you have a spouse whom you think will live longer than you, enter the age you would have been at the time of his or her death.)

The program will then calculate all your numbers each year from age 55 to 95 including —

- what your RRSP will be worth when you retire and every year thereafter;

- your required income, adjusted for inflation;

- CPP and OAS income, also adjusted for inflation;

- the amount of any OAS clawback;

- the minimum RRIF withdrawal amounts you will be required to make;

- the year-by-year RRSP and RRIF values, taking into account investment returns and withdrawals;

- how much your RRSP or RRIF will still be worth when you die; and

- the approximate personal income taxes that would be payable on the RRSP/RRIF value on your death.

Even if you are not that comfortable with computers, *Microsoft Excel,* or personal finance, I encourage you to give it a try — it can't hurt! If you are comfortable with it, keep it up-to-date by changing your inputs as your situation changes (for example, investment rates of return, inflation, percentage of income you will require after you retire).

8

MAKING THE RIGHT CHOICES BY USING THE RIGHT TOOLS

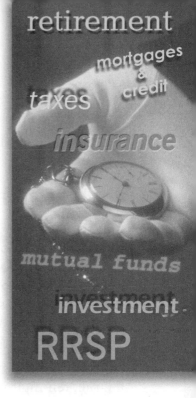

Now that you understand the myths that may be used to fool you out of your hard-earned money, you need to know what to do about it. How can you turn the tables, take control, and fight back?

KNOWLEDGE IS A TOOL

In the world of personal financial planning, as in most other parts of life, knowledge is key. It's difficult to dispute the messages you hear every day about what to do with your money if you don't understand what is being said.

If you haven't been trained in money matters for either your job or your own interest, you need to resolve now to devote some time to financial learning. Check out your library or local bookstore, subscribe to a magazine, and follow the financial writers in your favourite daily newspaper. (I read Ellen Roseman's and James Daw's columns in the *Toronto Star* religiously.)

Just get interested. If you don't, you are a sitting duck against the slick messages launched at you by the multi-million dollar advertising arms of the big financial institutions.

YOUR BEST FRIEND: A BUSINESS CALCULATOR

In addition to knowledge, there is one tool you will find indispensable in your quest for financial freedom: a good business calculator. It will allow you to experiment with different scenarios in saving for retirement as well as to calculate all the variables in any type of loan arrangement.

You can purchase a business calculator at any well-stocked business or stationery store. Look for one that has a large, ten-digit readout and which comes with an instruction manual. This inexpensive item (you can expect to pay about $30 to $50) will be worth its weight in gold. It will allow you to calculate future value of money, compounding interest rates, and much more. You'll also find that they are easy to learn how to use. Just follow the instructions that come with the model you choose. (Also see the box on pages 120 and 121 for more information on the basics of using a business calculator.)

Calculating the Future: Example

Here's a simple example that will show you how having a business calculator in your back pocket can help you fight back with both knowledge and tools:

Allyson and Sue are both 22 years old. They have both heard the sales pitch: "Start saving now for retirement or else!"

Allyson buys into the pitch and invests $2,000 a year for six years, and then she stops when she quits her job to stay home for a few years with her small child.

Sue, on the other hand, chooses to spend some of her money on herself for a few years. She travels around the world and works in a variety of jobs before settling down. She starts investing seven years later, and she, too invests $2,000 a year, but she manages to do so for the next 37 years.

Both women earn 12 percent on their investments. When Allyson and Sue reach age 65, who will be further ahead? The one who started early and interrupted her savings plan, or the one who waited a few years? With a business calculator, you can find the answer easily.

- For Allyson, you first need to calculate the future value of the annuity of $2,000 per year for six years. Answer: $16,230.38. Then you need to calculate the future value of that single amount for 37 years. Answer: $1,074,967.98.

- For Sue, you need to calculate the future value of an annuity of $2,000 for 37 years. Answer: $1,087,197.38.

As you can see, both women end up with about $1 million, but Sue comes out a little bit ahead over 43 years (by $12,229.40).

Without a business calculator, it's very difficult to make these calculations and even harder to argue with a salesperson who is trying to convince you that one strategy is better than another. But with a business calculator in hand, you've got the power to check the figures and, more importantly, to plug in your own figures. After all, it's your figures that count, not a canned example.

For instance, forget about a 12 percent annual return. What happens if it's only 5 percent? The future value in both cases is only about $203,000 — a lot less appealing.

The Low Monthly Lease Trap

With a business calculator, you can protect yourself against a devious method of consistently draining your bank account: the low monthly lease trap.

Whether it's cars, couches, appliances, or computers, consumers are constantly bombarded by ads for high-priced items promoting low monthly lease payments. It's all so painless isn't it? In some cases they don't even tell you the cost of the item. Without knowing the cost, it's virtually impossible to determine whether you're getting a good deal or not. Leasing is one of the ways companies can play games and record a handsome profit without your even knowing you've been taken.

You may have heard an old rule of thumb that you should buy things that appreciate and lease things that depreciate. If this were the case, you would always lease everything from a car to a computer because they decline in value over time.

Unfortunately, it's not that simple. The answer totally depends on the specifics of the situation. Let's look at the example of a computer.

If you lease a computer, you'll have to give it back at the end of the lease or buy it out. If you purchase it, it's yours to keep. Before you even consider the numbers, think about the difference in those two options. After two or three years your computer will be very outdated. If you run a business that requires current technology, you'll need a new one. Who is going to use the old one? The kids? Forget it; they probably need more power than you to run all their games and peripherals. When you get a new one, you probably won't even touch the old one again. Face it: your old computer is a boat anchor. If it's going to be that useless, why buy it? Leasing seems like the obvious answer, but is it?

Let's look at a real-life example of what it may cost to lease. Here are the facts:

- Estimated cost: $3,458.00
- Lease term: 36 months
- Monthly lease payment: $127.78
- Estimated purchase option price at end of lease term: fair market value

The last point is the wild card. What is the fair market value going to be after three years? They don't say in the contract, but in a previous lease it was 15 percent of the cost, so we'll assume it's $518.70 ($3,458 x 15%).

The important point to note with leases is that since you don't own the item in the end, you are not financing the whole cost of the item. You have to discount the end-of-lease buyout amount (at the incremental cost of borrowing). The present value of $518.70 at a discount rate of, say, 5 percent, is $448.07.

In this case, you are financing only $3,009.93 ($3,458.00 – $448.07). On your business calculator, you can compute the internal rate of return that this lease is costing:

- The present value is 3,009.93.
- The number of payments is 36.
- The payment amount is $127.78.

The monthly interest cost is 2.5 percent. The annual interest rate is a whopping 30 percent (2.5 x 12).

The interest amount over the 36-month term is the difference between the total payments of $4,600.08 (36 x $127.78) and the amount being financed ($3,009.93).

In all, that's $1,590.15 in interest over three years for the use of the computer, and you don't even own it at the end!

Look at it another way. If you took out a loan to purchase this computer at a rate of 7 percent a year, your monthly payments would be only $106.77, and you would then own it.

The moral of the story is to beware. Leasing can be very deceiving, and a business calculator won't let you down!

The Basics of Using a Business Calculator

Finance is based on the concept of the time value of money. A dollar in your hands today is worth more than a dollar you'll get a year from now. The underlying basis for any calculation concerning the time value of money is rate of return.

Here are the terms and abbreviations with which you should become familiar to use your business calculator:

- PV: present value of money
- FV: future value of money
- i: interest rate per compounding period
- n: number of compounding periods
- PMT: the payment amount (for a series of payments)

Let's look at how these terms plug into two examples:

Example: The Power of Compounding

If you have $100 today and you put the money into a term deposit earning 5 percent per year, you will have $105 at the end of the year. That's $100 in principal, plus $5 in interest. In this case, the present value (PV) is $100, the interest rate (i) is 5 percent per year (or per annum), the compounding period (n) is 1, and the future value (FV) is $105.

Put another way, the present value of a future value of $105 discounted at a rate of 5 percent for one year is $100.

In most cases, you will be dealing with more than one period in your calculations, and that's where the concept of compounding comes in. Compounding refers to how often

---

the interest amount comes into the calculation. Say you invested the $100 for 5 years at 5 percent per year. At the end of the first year, you would have $105; but at the end of the second year, you would have $110.25 since the $105 at the end of the first year would be earning 5 percent for the second year. That's $5.25; $5.00 on the principal of $100 and $0.25 on the $5 of interest.

The third year, you'd have $115.76; the fourth, $121.55; and at the end of five years, you would have $127.63.

Example: Breaking Down the Figures

Assume you are going to buy a car. The cost, including all freight, duty, taxes, and shipping, is $22,000. The sales rep says, "Congratulations. You're approved! Your payments are $502.09 a month for five years."

A good deal? Your business calculator will let you know:

- Enter 22,000, then "PV" (present value of the purchase)
- Enter 60, then "n" (12 payments per year for 5 years = the number of compounding periods)
- Enter 502.09, then "+/-" then "PMT" (Remember, money going out is negative.)
- Select "COMP," then "i"

Your calculator should display the monthly interest rate of 1.09 percent. Multiply that by 12 to get the annual rate, which is 13.08 percent. Show that to the sales rep, and then get back to negotiating a better rate or go elsewhere!

9

YOUR MORTGAGE:
FRIEND OR FOE?

If you're like most people, you probably think that you should try to reduce your expenses so you can spend more on the things you want and save for a decent retirement. There are many who argue that the way to do this is to reduce your daily expenses. Skip that cup of Tim Hortons coffee on the way to work. Forget that trip to the zoo and let the kids play in the backyard instead. Pack a lunch rather than buying one.

Is this really an effective strategy? Surely there's a better way than eliminating all the small indulgences that make life a little brighter. Instead, why not give some thought to the biggest expenses you'll ever have and reduce them instead?

Your mortgage is probably going to be the most significant debt you will ever incur. The decisions you make regarding your mortgage will, therefore, have a huge impact on your financial situation. The problem is that the various options are confusing, and as a result people often just accept whatever their bank offers. Don't do this. You could be throwing away thousands, perhaps even tens of thousands, of your hard-earned dollars.

Mortgage Terminology

Amortization: The gradual reduction in the principal balance owing, which happens because of the partial payments of principal plus interest at regular intervals.

Amortization period: The time required to pay off the principal balance through regularly scheduled repayments.

Blended payment: Each payment contains amounts for both principal and interest, which change over time while the overall payment remains the same.

Conventional mortgage: A first mortgage for which the amount loaned does not exceed 75 percent of the appraised value of the property.

High-ratio mortgage: A mortgage that exceeds 75 percent of the appraised value of the property. It must be insured to protect the lender in case of default by the borrower.

Interest: The amount paid by the borrower (mortgagor) to the lender (mortgagee) for the use of the money.

Maturity date: The final date in the term of the debt (not the amortization period).

Principal: The amount payable to the financial institution that gave you the mortgage. It begins with the total amount you borrow and is reduced by the principal portion of each payment.

Term: The period of time during which the money is loaned at a certain interest rate. This is usually six months or one, two, three, four, or five years.

MORTGAGE BASICS

To understand the essential elements of a mortgage, let's start with a simple example and work through the different components.

Say you bought a house for $200,000 using $50,000 of your own money and borrowing the remaining $150,000. That means the opening principal balance of the mortgage would be $150,000.

Assume the mortgage was at a 5 percent annual interest rate for a five-year term and was being amortized over 25 years. The bank tells you that your monthly payments are $872.41. Is that right? You won't know unless you have an amortization schedule.

Using an Amortization Schedule

An amortization schedule is a detailed spreadsheet that shows the interest and principal portion of each payment for the entire life of a mortgage. You will need to know the following to produce an accurate amortization schedule:

- Interest rate
- Term
- Amortization period
- Compounding method (daily, monthly, semi-annually, annually, etc.)

You can produce an amortization schedule by using a basic software program that will print out a full amortization schedule for any period — even a 30-year mortgage. It shows all details to the penny and is flexible enough to include special payments at any time. If you have an amortization software program, you will be able to compare alternatives before choosing a mortgage, and that can potentially save you a lot of money.

Don't use the amortization "quick and dirty" calculators found on a myriad of financial websites. It's worth investing in a proper program that allows you to plug in different interest rates, amortization periods, and monthly payments to see which option suits you best. (The program

I have been using for years is an excellent one called *MORTGAGE2 PRO*. It was written by a Canadian engineer, Ron Cirotto, and is available through his website at <www.amortization.com>.)

Key Mortgage Variables

There are several key variables in a mortgage to consider. Figure 3, a screen shot from the first page of the amortization schedule for our example, illustrates these.

Figure 3
MORTGAGE AMORTIZATION SCHEDULE

Date	Days	Pmt #	Payment	Int %	Interest	Principal	Balance	Prepay	Acc. Int	Notes
2/1/2004	31	1	872.41	5.0000	618.59	253.82	149,746.18	.00	618.59	
3/1/2004	29	2	872.41	5.0000	617.54	254.87	149,491.31	.00	1,236.13	
4/1/2004	31	3	872.41	5.0000	616.49	255.92	149,235.39	.00	1,852.62	
5/1/2004	30	4	872.41	5.0000	615.43	256.98	148,978.41	.00	2,468.05	
6/1/2004	31	5	872.41	5.0000	614.37	258.04	148,720.37	.00	3,082.42	
7/1/2004	30	6	872.41	5.0000	613.31	259.10	148,461.27	.00	3,695.73	
8/1/2004	31	7	872.41	5.0000	612.24	260.17	148,201.10	.00	4,307.97	
9/1/2004	31	8	872.41	5.0000	611.17	261.24	147,939.86	.00	4,919.14	
10/1/2004	30	9	872.41	5.0000	610.09	262.32	147,677.54	.00	5,529.23	
11/1/2004	31	10	872.41	5.0000	609.01	263.40	147,414.14	.00	6,138.24	
12/1/2004	30	11	872.41	5.0000	607.92	264.49	147,149.65	.00	6,746.16	
1/1/2005	31	12	872.41	5.0000	606.83	265.58	146,884.07	.00	7,352.99	
2/1/2005	31	13	872.41	5.0000	605.74	266.67	146,617.40	.00	7,958.73	
3/1/2005	28	14	872.41	5.0000	604.64	267.77	146,349.63	.00	8,563.37	
4/1/2005	31	15	872.41	5.0000	603.53	268.88	146,080.75	.00	9,166.90	
5/1/2005	30	16	872.41	5.0000	602.42	269.99	145,810.76	.00	9,769.32	
6/1/2005	31	17	872.41	5.0000	601.31	271.10	145,539.66	.00	10,370.63	
7/1/2005	30	18	872.41	5.0000	600.19	272.22	145,267.44	.00	10,970.82	
8/1/2005	31	19	872.41	5.0000	599.07	273.34	144,994.10	.00	11,569.89	

Figure 3, MORTGAGE2 PRO, copyright © 2003 is used by permission of Ron Cirotto.

You can see under the "payment" column that the first monthly blended payment is $872.41, which consists of $618.59 in interest and $253.82 in principal. The "balance" column shows that there is $149,746.18 remaining on the mortgage after that first payment (the original balance of

$150,000 less the $253.82 principal portion of the first payment).

Total Interest

Now look at the line just above all the columns in Figure 3. There you will see the total interest that you would pay on this mortgage for the entire amortization period. It's $111,721.44. That figure is key in mortgage comparisons because it summarizes the big picture — exactly what the mortgage will cost you over its life.

Effective Interest Rate

Amortization programs can also show the effective interest rate (EIR). In Figure 3, you can see it to the right of the annual interest rate: an EIR of 5.0625. But why is it higher than 5 percent, the annual interest rate of the mortgage? The answer has to do with compounding frequency.

Canadian residential mortgages are stated at an annual interest rate with semi-annual compounding. By law, they can't be compounded more frequently than that. The compounding period is six months, while the repayment period is usually monthly or biweekly, which results in an effective annual interest rate being higher than the annual interest rate.

Let's look at the 5 percent annual rate used in the example. For the first six months, you pay 5 percent x 6/12 which is 2.5 percent, so the factor is 1.025 percent for that period. For the next six months, you would pay 2.5 percent on the 1.025 percent, and that's 1.025 x 1.025, which equals 1.050625. The annual effective interest rate is therefore 1.050625 minus 1, which equals 5.0625 percent.

Remember that the compounding frequency is the number of times during a period, usually a year, that the interest component comes into the transaction. With investments, you are better off with more frequent compounding, because the interest you have earned in the first compounding period (but haven't received yet) is added to the investment principal balance, and the interest for the next period is calculated on the combination of the two.

With mortgages the opposite is true. The lender is the investor and you are the borrower. Sorry, you lose.

Days Per Year

Another key factor in mortgage calculations is the days per year. Everyone knows there are 365 days in a year and 366 in a leap year; but with a mortgage, you can select either 360 or 365 (see the box in the upper right-hand corner in Figure 3). The reason for selecting 360 days is that in banking circles, the year is often divided into 12 equal 30-day months. The total is 360.

In Canada prior to 1984, almost all mortgages were monthly payment mortgages using a 360-day year. After 1984, weekly and biweekly payment mortgages were introduced and along with that came another method of calculating mortgages: the exact day monthly payment mortgage which uses a 365-day year.

The major banks in Canada offer both 360- and 365-day payment amortizations, but often don't tell you which method they are using. Before making a decision about which mortgage to accept you should know.

One way to find out is to ask them for an amortization schedule. It will answer your question. The monthly interest factor for a 360-day schedule is constant from month to month and therefore the interest portion of the blended payment decreases consistently each period. The monthly interest factor for a 365-day schedule is dependent on the number of days from one month to the next and thus it changes each month.

In most cases the number of days per year does not have a significant effect on the overall interest cost of the mortgage, but knowing which method is being used will allow you to figure out the interest cost of each payment to the penny. That's what you need to do for effective personal financial tracking. (See Chapter 10.)

HOW TO SAVE MONEY WITH YOUR MORTGAGE

Once you understand how to assess the variables in a mortgage, you are ready to calculate how you can save a lot of money by making an effective mortgage decision. The interest rate is the place to start, and that depends on the term you select.

Choose the Right Term

Generally, the longer the term of the mortgage, the higher the interest rate you are going to pay. You pay a premium to lower the risk that mortgage rates are going to rise above the interest rate you've negotiated during the term. In Canada, you can choose from variable rate, six-month, or one-, two-, three-, four-, five-, seven-, and ten-year terms. A recent check showed a six-month mortgage rate that was 1.5 percent lower than for a 10-year term.

If you choose a shorter term, you could save big. This is illustrated in Figure 4, which shows the average monthly residential mortgage rates for one-year and five-year mortgages since 1980.

In Figure 4, note the following:

- The average one-year rate was 9.35 percent, and the average five-year rate 10.49 percent, for a difference of 1.14 percent;

- The lowest one-year rate was 4.43 percent in 2004, and the lowest five-year rate was 6.15 percent, also in 2004;

Figure 4
CONVENTIONAL MORTGAGE INTEREST RATES
SINCE 1980

Date	1-YEAR	5-YEAR	DIFFERENCE
1980	13.98	14.52	-0.54
1981	18.13	18.38	-0.25
1982	16.85	18.04	-1.19
1983	10.98	13.23	-2.25
1984	12.00	13.58	-1.58
1985	10.31	12.13	-1.81
1986	10.15	11.21	-1.06
1987	9.85	11.17	-1.31
1988	10.83	11.65	-0.81
1989	12.85	12.06	0.79
1990	13.40	13.35	0.04
1991	10.08	11.13	-1.05
1992	7.87	9.51	-1.64
1993	6.91	8.78	-1.87
1994	7.83	9.53	-1.70
1995	8.38	9.16	-0.78
1996	6.19	7.93	-1.74
1997	5.54	7.07	-1.53
1998	6.50	6.93	-0.43
1999	6.80	7.56	-0.76
2000	7.85	8.35	-0.50
2001	6.14	7.40	-1.26
2002	5.17	7.02	-1.85
2003	4.84	6.39	-1.55
2004 (To June)	4.43	6.15	-1.72
Average	9.35	10.49	-1.14
Lowest (2004)	4.43	6.15	
Highest (1981)	18.13	18.38	

Source: Bank of Canada <www.bankofcanada.ca/en/interest-look.htm>

- The highest one-year rate was 18.13 percent in 1981, and the highest five-year rate was 18.38 percent in the same year.

This shows clearly that you pay a significant premium to stick to a five-year term. In fact, I ran the average interest rates for both the one- and five-year terms on our $150,000 mortgage, both with an amortization period of 25 years. Here's what came up:

- One-year rate of 9.35 percent: monthly payments of $1,276.60, and total interest of $232,983.27;

- Five-year rate of 10.49 percent: monthly payments of $1,391.47 and total interest of $267,446.84.

The 1.14 percent interest difference would cost you $34,463.57 in additional interest, enough to keep you going back to Tim Hortons for quite a while.

The Sleep Test

Despite what you can save with a short-term mortgage, it's not for everyone. You have to be able to live with the risk that interest rates may increase. The test is the effect on your sleep. Does the thought of not locking in your rate for five years keep you up at night? If it does, keep the long-term mortgage and avoid the permanent bags under your eyes.

Payment Frequency

Many people think that if they switch from monthly payments (12 times per year) to biweekly (26 payments per year), they will save a lot of interest. That's simply not true.

Let's look at the effect on our sample mortgage (see Figure 5). The only change is the number of payments per year, from 12 to 26. The program has calculated the biweekly payment to be $402.20. The total interest for the 26-payment mortgage is $111,432.36, compared to

$111,721.44 for the 12-payment mortgage — a savings of only $289.08.

Figure 5
AMORTIZATION SCHEDULE WITH BIWEEKLY PAYMENTS

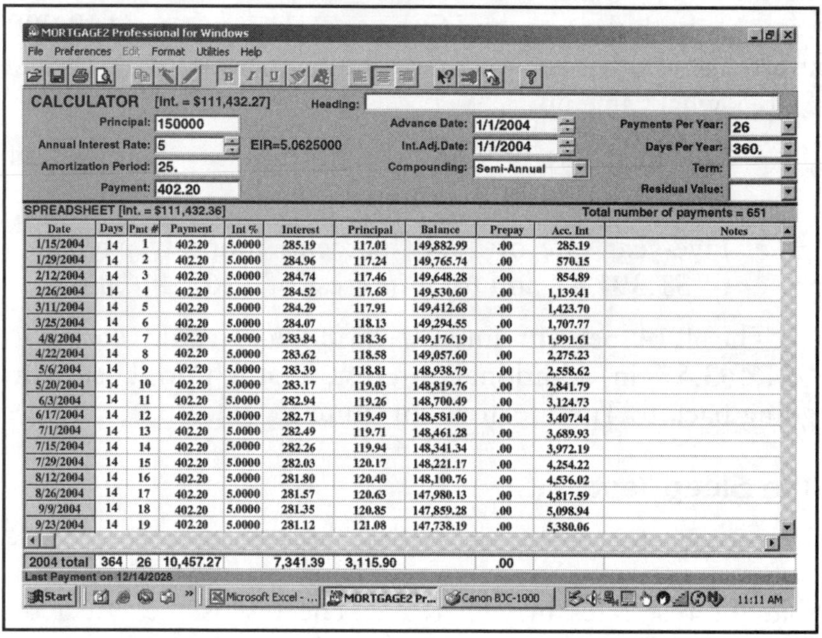

Date	Days	Pmt #	Payment	Int %	Interest	Principal	Balance	Prepay	Acc. Int	Notes
1/15/2004	14	1	402.20	5.0000	285.19	117.01	149,882.99	.00	285.19	
1/29/2004	14	2	402.20	5.0000	284.96	117.24	149,765.74	.00	570.15	
2/12/2004	14	3	402.20	5.0000	284.74	117.46	149,648.28	.00	854.89	
2/26/2004	14	4	402.20	5.0000	284.52	117.68	149,530.60	.00	1,139.41	
3/11/2004	14	5	402.20	5.0000	284.29	117.91	149,412.68	.00	1,423.70	
3/25/2004	14	6	402.20	5.0000	284.07	118.13	149,294.55	.00	1,707.77	
4/8/2004	14	7	402.20	5.0000	283.84	118.36	149,176.19	.00	1,991.61	
4/22/2004	14	8	402.20	5.0000	283.62	118.58	149,057.60	.00	2,275.23	
5/6/2004	14	9	402.20	5.0000	283.39	118.81	148,938.79	.00	2,558.62	
5/20/2004	14	10	402.20	5.0000	283.17	119.03	148,819.76	.00	2,841.79	
6/3/2004	14	11	402.20	5.0000	282.94	119.26	148,700.49	.00	3,124.73	
6/17/2004	14	12	402.20	5.0000	282.71	119.49	148,581.00	.00	3,407.44	
7/1/2004	14	13	402.20	5.0000	282.49	119.71	148,461.28	.00	3,689.93	
7/15/2004	14	14	402.20	5.0000	282.26	119.94	148,341.34	.00	3,972.19	
7/29/2004	14	15	402.20	5.0000	282.03	120.17	148,221.17	.00	4,254.22	
8/12/2004	14	16	402.20	5.0000	281.80	120.40	148,100.76	.00	4,536.02	
8/26/2004	14	17	402.20	5.0000	281.57	120.63	147,980.13	.00	4,817.59	
9/9/2004	14	18	402.20	5.0000	281.35	120.85	147,859.28	.00	5,098.94	
9/23/2004	14	19	402.20	5.0000	281.12	121.08	147,738.19	.00	5,380.06	
2004 total	364	26	10,457.27		7,341.39	3,115.90		.00		

Figure 5, MORTGAGE2 PRO, copyright © 2003 is used by permission of Ron Cirotto.

Payment Amount

Simply increasing your payment frequency won't help much; increasing the payment *amount* will.

For example, the 12 monthly payments in our example of $872.41 total $10,468.92 in a year. If you were to make 24 payments (semi-monthly), you would pay $436.21 twice per month ($10,468.92/24). Use that amount for your 26 bi-weekly payments, and you are effectively making two extra payments each year. That will pay off your mortgage sooner and save a lot of interest.

Figure 6 shows the amortization schedule for 26 payments of $436.21. The total interest has declined to $93,588.65. That's $18,132.79 less than the regular monthly payment mortgage. Now you're saving money.

Figure 6
AMORTIZATION SCHEDULE WITH 26 PAYMENTS

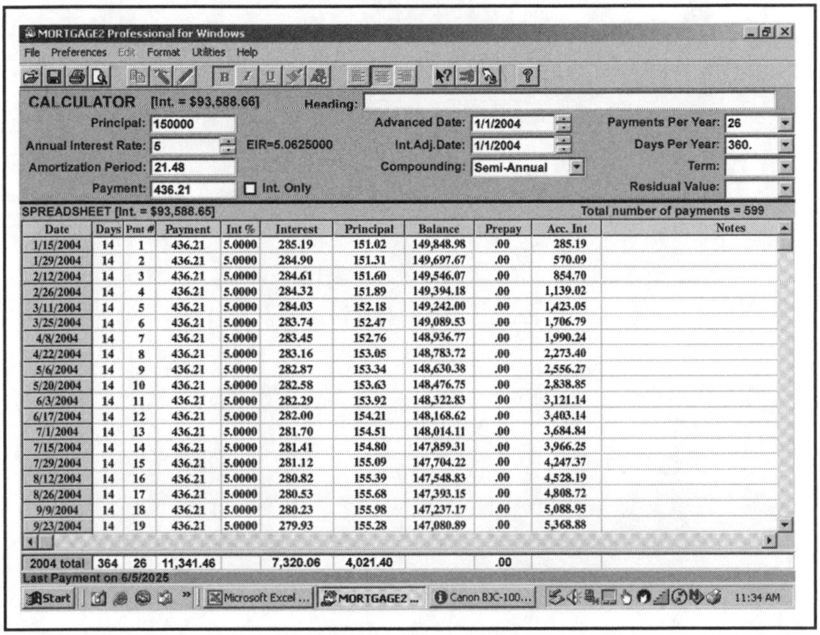

Figure 6, MORTGAGE2 PRO, copyright © 2003 is used by permission of Ron Cirotto.

10
TRACKING YOUR FINANCES: THE ULTIMATE WEAPON

Most people are very sloppy with their personal finances. They pay their bills and credit cards late, they rush major financial decisions, and their investments languish due to a lack of attention. This kind of behavior leads to —

- loss of thousands of dollars in needless interest and other charges,

- mounting debt levels,

- poorly performing investment portfolios,

- increased risk of a major financial meltdown, and

- ruined retirement dreams.

Your financial affairs don't have to follow this pattern. You *can* take control, stop the hemorrhaging, and begin to build a solid financial future. Unfortunately, it's not going to be easy, and it won't happen quickly. It takes years for most people to get into this kind of mess; it will take more than a few months to get out of it.

THE IMPORTANCE OF PERSONAL FINANCIAL TRACKING

The best way that you can take control of your finances is to spend time tracking and analyzing them. I call this process "personal financial tracking."

Personal financial tracking is the process of recording all income and expenses that your family incurs during the year as well as all the changing asset values and debt balances. Put simply, it's bookkeeping for your personal life.

It is no different than what any business must do. To succeed, a business needs accurate bookkeeping records of what has happened in the past and where it stands at the moment. In fact, every business is required to do this kind of bookkeeping in order to file income taxes.

It's really no different for personal finances. You have to report your income, but if you are employed, that is done for you by your employer on an annual basis. All you have to do is file your T4 slip with your personal income tax return. If you are self-employed, your business revenues and expenses must be reported.

The problem arises with your personal expenses. There is no outside force demanding that you track them, so if you're like most people, you probably just don't do it; and that's a huge mistake. If you don't know where the money is going, it's very difficult to spot and plug the big money leaks.

THE MOTIVATION TO GET STARTED

Of course, most people don't deliberately set out to get themselves into a financial mess. Tracking your finances takes time and commitment, and often there just doesn't seem to be enough hours in the day. For most people, life is busy enough with work and the demands of a family. Even those with the best intentions rarely get around to spending time on their personal finances. Many conclude that working harder to make more money will solve their financial problems. The result is that they have even less time available for what really matters in life, while excessive spending sucks the life out of their finances.

Often, another roadblock is that the information needed is disorganized or even missing. Without an efficient filing system, you're pretty well doomed from the start. I have dealt with hundreds of people over the years, and I usually find some consistent traits: those who have all their accounting records organized and on time one year usually do it every year. Those who are disorganized remain that way.

Unless you are very disciplined and organized, you are unlikely to naturally make positive changes. You need some motivation to start tracking, and that's not hard to find. If you start tracking your finances, odds are you'll find *at least* one area that is wasting your money. If you identify and plug one money drain, you could end up saving thousands of dollars.

At the very least, start a folder for each area of your personal finances: bank statements, RRSP statements, credit cards, and loans. That way, you can locate information to make some basic decisions. Maybe you will decide to move a balance from a gold credit card at 19 percent to a line of credit at 7 percent, or maybe you'll plan a vacation in Canada this year rather than an excursion to the South Pacific. Perhaps you'll buy a used car after your SUV lease expires.

Add up the savings, and it could work out to an after-tax windfall of thousands of dollars for several hours work.

Take my own example. Six years ago, I decided to get serious about tracking my own personal finances. I tried for months to get myself to do it. I had the software, the motivation, and our family records filed neatly. I just couldn't bring myself to start. I remember thinking that the last thing I felt like doing after a hard day's work analyzing clients' financial statements was cranking up the computer and filling up my spare time with a bookkeeping exercise.

What actually got me going wasn't any lofty goal; it was the motivation of money. I thought to myself that I would gladly pay someone, probably a bookkeeper, $100 per month to enter all our personal financial information into a spreadsheet program. Then it struck me: if I could learn how to do this efficiently, it could be a service that I could provide for a fee. That's when I buckled down and developed the system I describe in this chapter.

TRACKING HOTSPOTS

You can make your personal financial tracking easier if you recognize — and address — the hotspots. Those are the daily expenses that may seem small at the time, but can add up to huge amounts. These kinds of expenses are also very easy to forget about, and so they may not get tracked at all.

Expenses paid by cash are the most vulnerable to being "lost," and cash withdrawals are probably the biggest problem for people trying to bring their finances under control. How many times have you withdrawn $50 or $100 from the ATM and been shocked a few days later when there's nothing left in your account? If you don't know where your money is going, you will find it very difficult to reduce or stop the outflow.

Unless you are a sucker for punishment and enjoy keeping receipts for every little thing you buy in cash and then summarizing them later, use a debit card for as many expenses as possible. The payee's name will be included on the bank statement for every transaction, saving you the time of figuring out where your money went. Even if you don't remember exactly what the details of the transactions were, at least you will know which organization the money went to, and you'll be able to make an educated guess about in which expense category it belongs.

I also suggest that you write cheques whenever possible instead of using cash. Although not as easy as using a debit card, paying by cheque does provide a trail for your tracking purposes. For example, if you pay someone to cut your lawn, suggest paying by cheque instead of cash. When the bank returns your cheques with your monthly statement, you can record the expense appropriately.

PERSONAL FINANCIAL TRACKING OPTIONS

There are two methods for tracking your finances:

- The quick-and-dirty method
- The detailed tracking method

Let's look at each in turn.

The Quick-and-Dirty Method

The quick-and-dirty method is the easiest of the two, but is the least useful. Unfortunately, it's the method used by the majority of people who try to track their finances. Here's how it works:

Step 1: List your assets

First you list the balances of your assets as of a particular date. You can do this quite easily. Simply gather all your bank and investment statements, and estimate the value of your other assets, including your home, cars, and property (e.g., summer cottage), and list them all as of the same date. Use a month-end date, such as December 31. A worksheet is provided at the end of this chapter and on the CD-ROM for your convenience. (See Worksheet 1.)

Step 2: List your liabilities

The next step is to summarize the balances of all the amounts you owe as of the same date. Gather all credit card, mortgage, and other loan statements and list the amounts under your liabilities on Worksheet 1. Remember that liabilities are what you owe, so these are negative amounts.

Step 3: Calculate your net worth

Now subtract your total liabilities from your total assets. What you're left with is your net worth.

Step 4: Record your monthly income and expenses

Now you need to list your monthly income and expenses. To do so, you can use Worksheet 2 at the end of this chapter and on the CD-ROM. Start with the monthly amounts, then multiply by 12 to get the annual totals.

If you are on salary, your income figure is easy to determine: it's your net monthly pay. If you are self-employed, list the average amount you transfer each month to your personal bank account.

Listing your expenses accurately is the most difficult part of using this method. Some expenses are easier than others to determine. For example, you may have consistent monthly withdrawals for things like your mortgage, insurance, car payments, etc. Most other expenses, however, have to be estimated, and that is where problems can arise. Estimates are only guesses, and guesses are not a solid base from which to plan your financial future. For that reason, the quick-and-dirty method is the least accurate one to use.

The Detailed Tracking Method

This method tracks every dollar coming in and going out, which results in detailed reports of your spending and net worth. While it requires you to invest in a financial software program, the cost is easily offset by the time savings.

Having monthly details is far superior to estimating an average month and simply multiplying by 12 to get annual amounts. Because your finances will probably vary significantly from month to month, basing your annual estimate on one month will likely give you a false picture of what you are actually spending. Recording accurate historical information about your monthly spending will enable you to spot the cash drains. If you just guess, you are leaving those drains open.

The main software choices available are *Quicken* by Intuit and *Money* by Microsoft. These programs are designed to track personal finances and offer the following major advantages:

- You can automatically download bank and credit card information from your bank.

- You can generate extensive reports, allowing you to analyze things from a myriad of different angles.

- Automatic entries can be set up to save time.

- There are built-in loan amortization schedules.

- There is a built-in personal rate of return calculator for investments.

- Automatic double entry bookkeeping connects the cash flows to the related net worth accounts.

Downloading the transactions

Having the ability to download your banking information over the Internet directly to the program will save you hours of time.

Before you begin, you'll need to sign up for the service with your bank and select a password. Here are a few hints for effective tracking:

- Limit the number of bank accounts you have.

- Set up your credit cards for downloading as well.

- Always compare the balance in the bank account and credit card statement to the printed copy you receive in the mail to make sure you didn't miss anything.

A high-speed Internet connection is not imperative, because the download files are small. If you receive a message about the download being unsuccessful, just click through, as it often works anyway.

The main reports

The software will provide two main reports: the net worth report and the cash flow report.

The cash flow report shows you the amount of cash inflows and outflows during a period of time. The software program can either combine all sources, including bank accounts and credit cards, or it can "filter" the report to just show certain sources. It does all the work for you.

One of the most important reports is the cash flow comparison report. It gives a detailed listing of all income and expense categories for one period compared to another and calculates the amount difference. It is here that you will be surprised and possibly motivated to act by some of the categories. It is also here that you will experience the great feeling of making progress, as you increase income and decrease expense amounts.

It's important to note that the cash flow report includes transactions from all bank, cash, and credit card transactions, but excludes transfers between these accounts. For example, a transfer of $1,000 from your bank account to your credit card will not show on this report, nor would you want it to, as it is not an income or expense item but merely a transfer from one balance sheet account to another. The transfer will, of course, be reflected on the net worth statement, as the balance in your bank account and credit card accounts will have gone down by $1,000.

Investments

Unfortunately, unless you have an extraordinary broker, investment information won't be easy to enter, because you won't be allowed to download your information. Financial advisers also rarely show the cost of investments on monthly statements for reasons we have previously explored.

You will need to dig through your past files to find out how much you paid for each investment. Take the time to do this. If you don't, the reports on your investments will probably be misleading, and with your retirement at stake, you can't afford to be misinformed.

Separate amounts into components

It is very important to separate lump-sum payments into components. If you don't do this, you will get a skewed view of your expenses.

For example, your mortgage payments will have several parts. You need to separate the interest component (an expense) from the repayment of principal (a cash outflow that reduces a liability). The payment may also include property taxes (an expense).

The distinction is important, because the repayment of debt is quite different than the payment of either interest or property taxes. The repayment of debt is the progress you are making on getting out of debt. It reduces your liabilities on your statement of net worth.

To separate the principal reduction, you'll need an amortization schedule of the mortgage. You may have received one from your financial institution when you first took out or renewed your mortgage. If not, an amortization software program will do the job for you (see Chapter 9).

Salary deductions

The best way to deal with salary and employment income is to show the gross amount, and then list all the deductions separately. Doing so will provide you with the details on how much the various withholdings — such as income tax, CPP, and EI (employment insurance) — are costing you.

Interest

You should record interest expenses in a separate category for each loan. Doing so will make it easier to analyze your debt situation by highlighting exactly where the interest charges originate. You can then target and reduce the worst offenders first. When credit card interest stares you in the face for months on end, you may decide to do something about it!

Business expenses

If you are self-employed, create a separate category for expenses related to your business, even if you have a separate business bank account and bookkeeping records. There are many expenses that you incur personally which can also be claimed as business expenses, including automobile, meals and entertainment, and a home office. If you don't track these expenses, chances are they'll be missed, and that means you'll pay more tax than you should. Tracking also makes tax time easier for your accountant because the information is nicely summarized.

Children

You probably didn't decide to have kids based on a cash flow projection, but tracking how much they cost can help you to control these significant expenses. Make sure you separate the figures, such as before- and after-school programs, trips, camp, etc. Again, if you can't see these numbers, you'll find it difficult to keep them under control.

Household expenses

I suggest grouping together all home-related expenses. Doing so will give you the figures you need for any home-office deduction to which you may be entitled (if you have self-employment income), and it will also give you an over-all snapshot of how much your home is costing you. Consider categories for furniture, insurance, mortgage interest, property taxes (or rent), repairs and maintenance, security, and anything else you may have.

Insurance

Keep tabs on all types of insurance, including separate entries for life and disability insurance for you and your spouse. Insurance relating to personal and business automobiles, house, and business insurance should be placed under those categories.

PROJECTING INTO THE FUTURE

Tracking provides information about your past income and spending, but if you are to make changes, you need to look to the future. The personal finance software packages provide budgeting and cash flow features, but I have found them to be difficult to use. However, there is a solution. Simply export or copy the data to a spreadsheet such as Microsoft *Excel*.

The advantage to having your data in a spreadsheet is flexibility. It's easy to move things around and add columns where needed. If you are not familiar with spreadsheet use, I urge you to take a course on it. Once you learn how to use one, you'll find many uses for it in addition to budgeting.

Obviously, the first year is the toughest because you won't have any historical data on which to base your projections. Wait until you have at least a month or two of data in your file before doing any projecting. It's best to project your figures on an annual basis.

How to Use the Projection Spreadsheet

Have a look at Worksheet 3 at the end of this chapter and on the CD-ROM. It is a "projection" spreadsheet that will allow you to estimate your income and expenses for the rest of the year.

You will note that I have put income taxes and other deductions right under the gross income amounts on the spreadsheet, since doing so makes it easy to see the net amount available to spend. That is the figure that you need to keep in mind when you budget.

You will see several columns, as follows:

- Column B — Cash flow Actual 20x1
- Column C — Cash flow 1/1 - 3/31/20x2
- Column D — Cash flow 4/1 - 12/31/20x2
- Column E — Cash flow Estimate 20x2 (column C + column D)

Assume you have entered all your income and expense data in either *Quicken* or *Money* from January 1 to March 31 of year 20x2. Display the cash flow report for that period and either copy, export, or type in the actual totals into column C of the cash flow projection spreadsheet. Don't worry about column B for now. That's for the results of a prior year, once you have them.

Projecting the cash flows for the remainder of the year (column D) is made easier by the spreadsheet. Many income and expenses are monthly items, so if you have, say $180 in telephone expenses for the first three months of the year, put in $540 for the remaining nine months.

Hint: Put in a formula for the amount and copy to other categories that act the same. The formula is =C10/3*9 for the remainder of the year estimate if cell number C10 is the cell containing the $180 for three months' telephone expense.

Aim to update your personal finances at least every three months. Trying to do it more often will be difficult and won't really help much. If quarterly updates take too much time, try updating every six months. If you leave it for a year or more, it'll be too late to make any changes until the next year.

The main thing you will notice when you track your spending is that you probably have a significant amount of discretionary expenses — those things that aren't absolutely necessary. For example, you may see that those luxury car leases or that extended vacation are the easiest expenses to target and cut. Once you have detailed information on hand about your spending, you'll most likely be very surprised at the amount of money you can save.

A FEW WORDS ABOUT KILLER CREDIT CARDS

As I have said over and over, if you spend more than you make on a consistent basis, your financial situation will get worse and worse each day. Credit cards give you the instant ability to buy things that you can't afford. It's all so easy, but it can be deadly.

A gold card offering free air miles or merchandise may sound like a great deal, and it is, unless you don't pay off the balance in full by the due date. Interest rates of 19 percent up to 28 percent or more for some department store cards are common. The spending habits of many Canadians have given credit card companies a licence to print money, and they are experts at convincing you to load up the plastic.

Nonetheless, if you can afford to pay off your credit cards each month, they offer some great features.

If you find that you are too easily lured by the convenience of credit cards, try this: simply switch from a credit card to a debit card. This strategy will automatically limit your spending to what you have in the bank, plus any overdraft protection. I guarantee this will be tough if you carry a credit card balance from month to month, but the alternative is to keep spending more than you make by borrowing from the credit card company.

The use of credit cards is becoming an epidemic, with some companies even mailing out approved cards that have not even been requested, as well as targeting young people without jobs. Credit cards can be lifesavers, but they can also suck the financial life right out of you. Your best bet is to become educated about the traps.

The Financial Consumer Agency of Canada (FCAC) is an independent body started in 2001 to protect and educate consumers of financial products. Their website at <www.fcac-acfc.gc.ca/> has a tremendous amount of information concerning the use of credit cards.

They also have service fee tables that compare Visa, MasterCard, American Express, and various retail cards. They offer the following tips to help you save money with credit cards:

- Don't base your credit card decision on one factor such as the introductory rate or reward program. Look for the overall package that best suits your needs and financial situation.

- If possible, pay your entire balance in full each month. If you cannot pay the whole amount, transfer the balance to another form of credit with a lower interest rate such as a line of credit. If you do this every month you will benefit from the grace period on the card.

- If you carry a balance on a credit card, remember that interest is normally charged from the date a purchase is made until it is paid in full. Making early payments between statements will save you interest charges.

- Cash advances should be made only when absolutely necessary — for short-term or emergency situations, since interest is charged from the date you borrow until the advance is paid in full.

- Allow enough time for your payment to reach your credit card company.

- Consider the use of pre-authorized payment plans to automatically make your payments on time. You will need to keep track of such payments to make sure sufficient funds are in your account.

- Monitor your monthly statements for notices of fee increases or rule changes from your credit card company.

If you are carrying a balance on a gold or premium card charging you around 20 percent annual interest, your decision is not that tough. One option is to switch to a low-rate card. It's as easy as a phone call, in many cases. This switch will immediately save you around 10 percent a year in interest payments. The next step is tougher. How did you get here in the first place? You must have spent more than you earned over a period of time.

If you don't change your ways, even with a lower-rate card, the interest charges on an ever-increasing amount of credit card debt will eat your retirement dreams alive. The first step is to control yourself so that you are spending only what you make every year. Doing that will be tough, but it's the only way to stop the balance from rising.

Worksheet 1
NET WORTH STATEMENT

MY NET WORTH STATEMENT	
DATE:	$
ASSETS	
Cash and Bank Accounts	
Chequing account	
Savings account	
Total cash and bank accounts	
Other Assets (market value)	
Principal residence	
Cottage	
Auto 1	
Auto 2	
Total other assets	
Investments (market value)	
Business value	
Investment account 1	
Investment account 2	
RESP	
RRSP	
RRSP — Spouse	
Total investments	
TOTAL ASSETS	
LIABILITIES	
Credit Cards and Lines of Credit	
Credit card 1	
Credit card 2	
Line of credit	
Total credit cards and lines of credit	
Other Liabilities	
Principal residence mortgage	
Cottage mortgage	
Auto loan 1	
Auto loan 2	
Prior year personal taxes	
Total other liabilities	
TOTAL LIABILITIES	
NET WORTH (Assets — Liabilities)	

Worksheet 2
INCOME AND EXPENSES

MY INCOME AND EXPENSES	MONTH ($)	YEAR ($)
INCOME		
My net pay		
Self-employment income		
Spouse's net pay		
TOTAL INCOME		
EXPENSES		
Auto		
Fuel		
General		
Insurance		
Lease		
Licence & registration		
Loan interest		
Maintenance		
Total auto		
Business		
Advertising		
Auto fuel		
Auto insurance		
Auto lease		
Auto loan interest		
Auto maintenance		
Auto parking		
Auto other		
Dues & subscriptions		
Internet		
Loan interest		
Meals & entertainment		
Office & general		
Total business		

Worksheet 2 — Continued

	MONTH ($)	YEAR ($)
Children		
Childcare		
Daycare		
Holiday & camp program		
Lessons		
Private school tuition		
Trips & other		
Total children		
Family		
Cash withdrawals		
Clothing		
Donations		
Entertainment		
Gifts given		
Groceries		
Vacations		
Total family		
Household		
Furniture		
Insurance		
Mortgage interest		
Property tax		
Repairs & maintenance		
Rent		
Total household		
Insurance		
Disability		
Life		
Life — spouse		
Total insurance		

Worksheet 2 — Continued

	MONTH ($)	YEAR ($)
Interest and bank charges		
Bank charges		
Credit card interest		
Line of credit interest		
Personal taxes interest		
Total interest and bank charges		
Medical		
Dental		
Medical expense		
Private health care		
Total medical		
Other Expenses		
Legal & professional fees		
Recreation		
Restaurants — personal		
RRSP admin fees		
Subscriptions		
Miscellaneous		
Total other expenses		
Utilities		
Cable TV		
Cleaning		
Electric		
Gas & oil		
Lawn & driveway		
Security		
Telephone		
Water		
Total utilities		
TOTAL EXPENSES		
INCOME LESS EXPENSE		

Worksheet 3
CASH FLOW PROJECTION

CASH FLOW PROJECTION WORKSHEET				
A	**B**	**C**	**D**	**E**
	Actual			Estimate
	20x1	1/1 - 3/31/20x2	4/1 - 12/31/20x2	20x2 (C + D)
INFLOWS				
My Salary (gross)				
Interest income				
Other income				
Salary spouse (gross)				
TOTAL INFLOWS				
My tax				
CPP contributions				
EI contributions				
Income tax				
Total my tax				
Spouse tax				
CPP contributions				
EI contributions				
Income tax				
Pension				
Total spouse tax				
Total tax				
My net pay				
Spouse net pay				
Net other				
NET INFLOWS				
EXPENSES				
Auto				
Fuel				
General				
Insurance				
Lease				
Licence & registration				
Loan interest				
Maintenance				
Total auto				

Worksheet 3 — Continued

A	B	C	D	E
	Actual			Estimate
	20x1	1/1 - 3/31/20x2	4/1 - 12/31/20x2	20x2 (C + D)
Business				
Advertising				
Auto fuel				
Auto insurance				
Auto lease				
Auto loan interest				
Auto maintenance				
Auto parking				
Auto other				
Dues & subscriptions				
Internet				
Loan interest				
Meals & entertainment				
Office & general				
Total business				
Children				
Childcare				
Daycare				
Holiday & camp program				
Lessons				
Private school tuition				
Trips & other				
Total children				
Family				
Cash withdrawals				
Clothing				
Donations				
Entertainment				
Gifts given				
Groceries				
Vacations				
Total family				
Household				
Furniture				
Insurance				

Worksheet 3 — Continued

A	B	C	D	E
	Actual			Estimate
	20x1	1/1 - 3/31/20x2	4/1 - 12/31/20x2	20x2 (C + D)
Mortgage interest				
Property tax				
Repairs & maintenance				
Rent				
Total household				
Insurance				
Disability				
Life				
Life — spouse				
Total insurance				
Interest and bank charges				
Bank charges				
Credit card interest				
Line of credit interest				
Personal taxes interest				
Total interest and bank charges				
Medical				
Dental				
Medical expense				
Private health care				
Total medical				
Other expenses				
Legal & professional fees				
Recreation				
Restaurants — personal				
RRSP admin Fees				
Subscriptions				
Total other expenses				
Utilities				
Cable TV				
Cleaning				
Electric				
Gas & oil				
Lawn & driveway				

Worksheet 3 — Continued

A	B	C	D	E
	Actual			Estimate
	20x1	1/1 - 3/31/20x2	4/1 - 12/31/20x2	20x2 (C + D)
Security				
Telephone				
Water				
Total utilities				
TOTAL EXPENSES				
TRANSFERS				
TO Mortgage				
TO Investment a/c 1				
TO Investment a/c 2				
TO RESP				
TO Business loan				
TO My RRSP				
TO Spouse's RRSP				
TOTAL TRANFERS				
TOTAL OUTFLOWS (Expenses + Transfers)				
NET INFLOWS LESS TOTAL OUTFLOWS				

11

SUMMARY: WHAT YOU'VE LEARNED AND WHAT TO DO NEXT

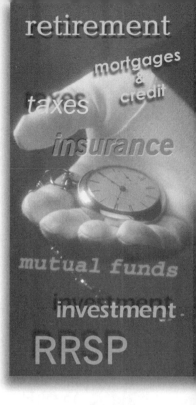

Now that we've exploded the top five myths about financial planning in Canada today, you're in a better position. Simply knowing what the myths are is an important first step in your quest to gain control of your finances and enjoy the trip to retirement and beyond.

A BRIEF OVERVIEW

Let's review the key points of each myth and the counter arguments to each.

- **Myth 1: If I Had a $1,000,000.00. . . I Could Retire:** The rule of thumb says you'll need at least 70 percent, perhaps even up to 100 percent, of your pre-retirement income after you retire, and that means you will need to save more than $1 million before you get there. Here's what we discovered as we took a journey with the Harts:

Reality: You probably won't need 70 percent, because you won't have the same level of expenses and you won't still be putting away money for retirement. You'll have at your disposal funds from your RRIF (converted from your RRSPS) as well as CPP and OAS to rely on. As well, if you manage to pay off your home mortgage, you've secured an excellent way of providing for your future. If you control your expenses and pay off all personal debt, you may need only 40 percent of your current income to retire comfortably.

- **Myth 2:** RRSPs **are the Holy Grail of Retirement:** Ask your average investment adviser about retirement, and he or she is likely to immediately jump into a discussion about your RRSP and how the stock market is the place to be, even if you have to borrow to invest. You'll likely be told how RRSPs can save you lots in taxes, too.

  Reality: Investing in RRSPs gives you a tax deduction now, but you have to pay tax on the withdrawals later. If your tax bracket is not much lower after you retire, the savings may not be much at all — perhaps only 3 percent or less. The real advantage to RRSPs is that they *defer* tax. That can be a real economic benefit, and that's one of the reasons why investing in RRSPs should be a part of your retirement planning — after all debt, including your mortgage, is paid off. Borrowing to invest in an RRSP is not wise. The only winner is the bank.

- **Myth 3: Don't Worry about Your Investments; You'll Be Fine in the Long Run:** The stock markets can give you a good return on your money. All you have to do is pick the right time to get in and the right time to get out.

  Reality: Choosing the right time to buy and sell in the stock market is almost impossible. You need to be very lucky to get it right. You're gambling with your future if you're counting on the stock market to provide you with your retirement funds. Use the personal rate of return calculator that comes on the CD-ROM with this book to figure out how well the stock market has done for you in the past before trusting it in the future.

- **Myth 4: We Have Met the Enemy, and He Is the Tax Collector:** Paying taxes is distasteful, but you can avoid doing so if you just pick the right tax shelter and use leverage to buy into a great investment.

  Reality: It doesn't make economic sense to invest $10,000 in a tax shelter to save $4,600, if there is little chance of getting your original investment back. If you don't get it back, you have just burned $5,400. It could even get worse if the government discovers that your tax shelter is a scam. And using "leverage" to get rich is as risky as it gets. You borrow money and hope that the returns will exceed the tax-deductible interest on the debt. You could get lucky and beat the odds, but you may very well end up broke if you choose the wrong investment or simply get the timing wrong.

- **Myth 5: Secure Your Financial Future: Buy Life Insurance:** Everyone needs insurance, and you can kill two birds with one stone if you invest in a policy that includes savings features.

  Reality: Insuring the life of the breadwinner in a family is a prudent step in personal financial planning. If he or she was to die, any dependants would be left with no means of sustaining themselves. However, insuring the life of someone who does not contribute economically to the family finances or someone without dependants is probably not necessary. Whole life insurance means a whole lot of commission to your insurance agent. That is one of the reasons why it is not a great way for you to save money. And your savings, otherwise known as the cash surrender value, helps fund the death benefit. You don't get the cash surrender value and the death benefit; you get one or the other.

You don't have to fall for these myths. You now have at your disposal the tools and weapons you'll need to defend yourself against those who wish to relieve you of your hard-earned money. You can use a business calculator to test investment projections and loan alternatives. You can work diligently to pay off what is probably your biggest personal debt: your home mortgage. And you can start using the ultimate weapon: personal financial tracking, the key to your financial well-being. If you can get yourself motivated to track your finances, you are armed and ready to defend yourself.

WHAT NOW?

Okay. You're not going to fall for any of the myths, you're committed to doing your own personal financial tracking from now on, you're going to attack all personal debt and pay it off as soon as possible, and you've successfully cut your expenses to the bone. What next?

Since you now pay your credit cards off in full each month, get the card with the most rewards for what you need and put everything on that card. It's like getting a free loan and being rewarded for taking it. Just don't fall into the trap. The credit card pit can be mighty deep, and it has very slippery walls.

Since all your debt is paid off, you'll have a lot of excess cash each month. Begin investing in earnest. Decide the best amount to put into your RRSP using the retirement optimizer that comes on the CD-ROM with this book. Spend time educating yourself about investing.

Oh, and take that dream vacation. You've earned it!